Instructions:

You don't have to know the names of any parts of speech to do well on the SAT, but a few basic terms are needed for you to understand explanations. Those terms are defined on some of these cards. Other cards offer a sentence with six highlighted words; test yourself by trying to identify what part of speech each represents.

Knowing the forms and proper uses of the six basic verb tenses will help you to score well in SAT Writing, so those are also here.

Knowing your idioms is essential; we've collected over 100 of those most commonly tested on the SAT.

Irregular verb forms are frequently tested. We include 72; can you name the past and perfect forms?

ADJECTIVE

ADVERB

ANTECEDENT

CLAUSE

CONJUNCTION

A word that modifies a noun or pronoun

My <u>lucky</u> brother had an <u>enormous</u> milkshake.

The noun or word group that a pronoun replaces

<u>Mary</u> was so happy she laughed uncontrollably.

A word that modifies a verb, adjective, or adverb

He was <u>very</u> disappointed that the game ended so quickly.

A word that connects words or groups of words

Maya <u>and</u> Bart walked to the park <u>and</u> fed the birds.

A group of words containing a subject and verb

<u>We</u> <u>went</u> to the stadium.

DEPENDENT CLAUSE

GERUND

INDEPENDENT CLAUSE

INFINITIVE

NOUN

OBJECT

A verb form ending in –*ing* that is used as a noun

Running is good exercise.

A clause that cannot stand alone as a sentence

Because he was too late, Tommy missed the bus.

A verb form preceded by *to* that is used as a noun or modifier

To swim by moonlight is a rare treat.

A clause that can stand alone as a sentence

Because he was too late, Tommy missed the bus.

Who or what is affected by the action in a sentence

She hit the ball so hard it split in two.

A word that represents a person, place, or thing

The boy was unable to complete the race in the time allowed.

PARTICIPLE

PHRASE

Grammar Basics

Grammar Basics

PRONOUN

PREPOSITION

Grammar Basics

Grammar Basics

SUBJECT

VERB

A group of words not containing a subject and verb

Going <u>to the grocery store</u> <u>on the weekend</u> was a regular family outing.

A verb form, often ending in –*ing*, that is used as an adjective

<u>Running</u> too fast to stop, she collided with her teammate.

A word that shows the relation of a noun or pronoun to another word

I've wanted to go <u>to</u> Spain <u>for</u> a long time.

A word that takes the place of a noun or pronoun

Jen isn't quick, but <u>she</u> is reliable, <u>which</u> makes <u>her</u> the best choice for the job.

A word that expresses action or state of being

We never <u>found</u> the book that Jerry <u>lost</u> last week.

The person or thing about which something is said in a clause

<u>Amir</u> won't be in until late this afternoon.

Grammar Basics

Identify the part of speech of each underlined word.

<u>Some</u> of us <u>simply</u> <u>cannot be</u> <u>satisfied</u> with a poorly done job.

Grammar Basics

Identify the part of speech of each underlined word.

<u>I</u> <u>will have</u> <u>some</u> soup <u>in</u> a mug.

Grammar Basics

Identify the part of speech of each underlined word.

<u>Go</u> <u>down</u> the <u>stairs</u> slowly and <u>carefully</u>.

Grammar Basics

Identify the part of speech of each underlined word.

<u>Down</u> jackets are <u>especially</u> <u>appropriate</u> for the <u>arctic</u> climate.

Grammar Basics

Identify the part of speech of each underlined word.

No <u>down</u> <u>payment</u> is necessary for <u>this</u> credit <u>purchase</u>.

Grammar Basics

Identify the part of speech of each underlined word.

I <u>am</u> certain that <u>this</u> <u>is</u> the <u>right</u> house.

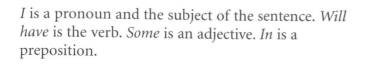

I is a pronoun and the subject of the sentence. *Will have* is the verb. *Some* is an adjective. *In* is a preposition.

Some is a pronoun and the subject of the sentence. *Simply* is an adverb modifying the verb *cannot be*. *Satisfied* is an adjective modifying *Some*.

Down is an adjective modifying the noun *jackets*. *Especially* is an adverb modifying the adjective *appropriate*. *Arctic* is an adjective modifying *climate*.

Go is the verb. *Down* is an adverb. *Stairs* is a noun. *Carefully* is an adverb modifying *go*.

Am is the main verb. *This* is a pronoun referring to the noun *house*. *Is* is the verb in the dependent clause "that this is the right house." *Right* is an adjective modifying *house*.

Down is an adjective modifying the noun *payment*. *This* is an adjective modifying *purchase*.

Grammar Basics

Identify the part of speech of each underlined word.

Please <u>light</u> the <u>oven</u> <u>or</u> dinner won't be <u>ready</u> on time.

Grammar Basics

Identify the part of speech of each underlined word.

The package was <u>too</u> <u>light</u> to be the <u>books</u> I <u>ordered</u>.

Grammar Basics

Identify the part of speech of each underlined word.

No <u>light</u> <u>penetrated</u> the <u>gloom</u> <u>of</u> the forest.

Grammar Basics

Identify the part of speech of each underlined word.

The principal <u>let</u> the students <u>leave</u> <u>early</u> <u>today</u>.

Grammar Basics

Identify the part of speech of each underlined word.

It <u>will</u> <u>snow</u> tomorrow, <u>according to</u> the <u>weather</u> <u>report</u>.

Grammar Basics

Identify the part of speech of each underlined word.

The <u>snow</u> shovels were <u>specially</u> designed to make <u>lifting</u> <u>easy</u>.

Too is an adverb modifying the adjective *light*. *Books* is a noun. *Ordered* is a verb.

Light is the verb. *Oven* is a noun. *Or* is a conjunction joining two independent clauses. *Ready* is an adjective modifying the noun *dinner*.

Let is the main verb of the sentence. *Leave* is a verb modified by the adverb *early*. *Today* is a noun.

Light is a noun and the subject of the sentence. *Penetrated* is the verb, in the simple past tense. *Gloom* is a noun. *Of* is a preposition.

Snow is an adjective modifying the noun *shovels*. *Specially* is an adverb modifying the adjective *designed*. *Lifting* is a verb form used as a noun, which is modified by the adjective *easy*.

Will snow is the future tense of the verb *snow*. *According to* is a preposition. *Weather* is an adjective modifying the noun *report*.

Grammar Basics

Identify the part of speech of each underlined word.

<u>Snow</u> <u>covered</u> the <u>surrounding</u> <u>countryside</u>.

Grammar Basics

Identify the part of speech of each underlined word.

Amir <u>couldn't reach</u> the shelf, <u>for</u> <u>he</u> was <u>too</u> small.

Grammar Basics

Identify the part of speech of each underlined word.

Edward <u>asked</u> <u>what</u> was <u>for</u> <u>dinner</u>.

Grammar Basics

Identify the part of speech of each underlined word.

The prospector <u>filed</u> <u>his</u> <u>claim</u> <u>immediately</u>.

Grammar Basics

Identify the part of speech of each underlined word.

The <u>visiting</u> team members <u>claim</u> that <u>they</u> <u>won</u>.

Grammar Basics

Identify the part of speech of each underlined word.

<u>We</u> <u>had to clear</u> the hallway <u>for</u> the <u>emergency</u> team.

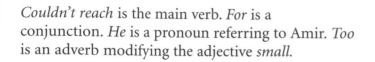

Couldn't reach is the main verb. *For* is a conjunction. *He* is a pronoun referring to Amir. *Too* is an adverb modifying the adjective *small*.

Snow is a noun, the subject of the sentence. *Covered* is the main verb in the past tense. *Surrounding* is an adjective modifying the noun *countryside*.

Filed is the main verb, modified by the adverb *immediately*. *His* is a pronoun referring to *the prospector. Claim* is a noun.

Asked is the main verb. *What* is a pronoun. *For* is a conjunction. *Dinner* is a noun.

We is a pronoun, the subject of the sentence. *Had to clear* is the verb. *For* is a preposition. *Emergency* is an adjective modifying team.

Visiting is an adjective modifying *members. Claim* is the main verb. *They* is a pronoun referring to *members. Won* is the verb in the dependent clause.

Grammar Basics

Identify the part of speech of each underlined word.

<u>By</u> late afternoon, it <u>became</u> <u>clear</u> that Geoff would finish <u>in</u> time.

Grammar Basics

Identify the part of speech of each underlined word.

He was <u>like</u> a swan <u>in</u> the water, but <u>but</u> a goose <u>on</u> the land.

Grammar Basics

Identify the part of speech of each underlined word.

I <u>didn't</u> <u>like</u> the way the barber <u>cut</u> the back <u>of</u> my <u>brother's</u> hair.

Grammar Basics

Identify the part of speech of each underlined word.

The <u>judges</u> couldn't be <u>objective</u> <u>in</u> <u>their</u> decision.

Grammar Basics

Identify the part of speech of each underlined word.

What is the <u>objective</u> <u>of</u> <u>this</u> <u>police</u> inquiry?

Grammar Basics

Identify the part of speech of each underlined word.

<u>When</u> we <u>saw</u> the jewelry, we had no <u>doubt</u> that he was the <u>culprit</u>.

Like, in, and on are all prepositions. *But* is a conjunction.

By is a preposition. *Became* is the main verb. *Clear* is an adjective. *In* is a prepositon.

Judges is a noun, the subject of the sentence, modified by the adjective *objective. In* is a preposition. *Their* is a pronoun referring to *the judges.*

Didn't like is the main verb. *Cut* is a verb in the dependent clause. *Of* is a preposition. *Brother's* is a possessive pronoun, which serves as an adjective.

When is an adverb modifying the verb *saw* (the past tense of the irregular verb *see*). *Doubt* is a noun, as is *culprit.*

Objective is a noun. *Of* is a preposition. *This* and *police* are adjectives modifying the noun *inquiry.*

Grammar Basics

Identify the part of speech of each underlined word.

Do you <u>doubt</u> <u>my</u> conclusion <u>about</u> the source <u>of</u> the water?

Grammar Basics

Identify the part of speech of each underlined word.

<u>Give</u> me <u>both</u> of the watches, <u>and</u> I'll get <u>them</u> repaired.

Grammar Basics

Identify the part of speech of each underlined word.

<u>Both</u> watches <u>must be</u> repaired <u>before</u> <u>next</u> Tuesday.

Grammar Basics

Identify the part of speech of each underlined word.

<u>Her</u> reply, <u>although</u> not what we expected, was <u>both</u> <u>timely</u> and correct.

Grammar Basics

Identify the part of speech of each underlined word.

<u>Fred's</u> test couldn't be graded; the <u>rest</u> <u>of</u> the class all <u>passed</u>.

Grammar Basics

Identify the part of speech of each underlined word.

We'll have to <u>rest</u> <u>before</u> we <u>continue</u> to <u>climb</u>.

Give is the verb in the first clause. *Both* is a pronoun. *And* is a conjunction joining two independent clauses. *Them* is a pronoun referring to *both of the watches.*

Doubt is the main verb. *My* is a possessive pronoun, which serves as an adjective. *About* is a preposition, as is *of.*

Her is a possessive pronoun used as an adjective modifying *reply. Although* is a conjunction introducing a dependent clause. *Both* is a conjunction, used with *and* to join the two adjectives. *Timely,* although it ends in *–ly,* is an adjective.

Both is an adjective modifying *watches. Must be* is the verb. *Before* is a preposition. *Next* is an adjective modifying Tuesday.

Rest is a verb. *Before* is a preposition. *Continue* is a verb, completed by the infinitive *to climb.*

Fred's is a possessive noun used as an adjective. *Rest* is a noun, the subject of the second independent clause. *Of* is a preposition. *Passed* is the verb in the second independent clause.

Grammar Basics

Identify the part of speech of each underlined word.

Despite our elaborate efforts, the baby wouldn't be still.

Grammar Basics

Identify the part of speech of each underlined word.

Spence is still the only photographer that I trust.

Grammar Basics

Identify the part of speech of each underlined word.

We used a still to produce distilled water for the experiment.

Grammar Basics

Identify the part of speech of each underlined word.

In the nineteenth century, toy soldiers were made of iron.

Grammar Basics

Identify the part of speech of each underlined word.

I never iron any of my shirts; I prefer them wrinkled.

Grammar Basics

Identify the part of speech of each underlined word.

A heavy Victorian iron fence with brass ornaments encircles my house.

Still is an adverb. *Only* is an adjective, despite its final *–ly*. *That* is a pronoun referring to *photographer*. *Trust* is a verb.

Despite is a preposition. *Elaborate* is an adjective modifying *efforts*. *Wouldn't be* is the main verb. *Still* is an adjective.

In is a preposition. *Toy* is an adjective modifying *soldiers*. *Were made* is the main verb. *Iron* is a noun.

Used is the main verb. *Still* is a noun. *Distilled* is a verb form used as an adjective modifying *water*. *For* is a preposition.

Heavy and *iron* are adjectives modifying *fence*. *With* is a preposition. *Brass* is an adjective modifying ornaments.

Iron is the verb in the first clause. *Any* is a pronoun. *Them* is a pronoun referring to shirts. *Wrinkled* is a verb form used as an adjective.

When do we use the

PRESENT TENSE

When do we use the

PAST TENSE

Grammar Basics

When do we use the

FUTURE TENSE

Grammar Basics

When do we use the

PRESENT PERFECT TENSE

Grammar Basics

When do we use the

PAST PERFECT TENSE

Grammar Basics

When do we use the

FUTURE PERFECT TENSE

Expresses action that occurred in the past

> I *went* home for the holidays.

> I *was going* home in a week.

> I *did go* to the store yesterday, but forgot the milk.

Expresses habitual action or action occurring at the present time

> John *dances* every day.

> Ada *is dancing* on stage.

> Janet *does dance* whenever she can.

Expresses action occurring at no definite time in the past or continuing into the present.

> You *have sold* more books than anyone else in the class.

> He *has been selling* candy bars since his sophomore year.

Expresses action that will occur sometime in the future.

> They will *sleep well* after this hard day's work.

> We *are going to sleep* in the boat tonight.

> We *will be sleeping* late tomorrow morning.

Expresses action completed before another event in the future.

> By the time we get home, my ice cream *will have melted*.

> By late spring, the snow *will have been melting* for several months.

Expresses action completed before some other past action

> When I *had spent* all my money, I had to ask for a loan.

Name the past and perfect form of:

ARISE

Name the past and perfect form of:

AWAKE

Name the past and perfect form of:

BEAR

Name the past and perfect form of:

BEAT

Name the past and perfect form of:

BEGIN

Name the past and perfect form of:

BITE

awake	awoke	awoke		arise	arose	arisen
beat	beat	beaten		bear	bore	borne
bite	bit	bitten		begin	began	begun

Name the past and perfect form of:

BLOW

Name the past and perfect form of:

BREAK

Name the past and perfect form of:

BRING

Name the past and perfect form of:

BUILD

Name the past and perfect form of:

BURST

Name the past and perfect form of:

BUY

break	broke	broken		blow	blew	blown
build	built	built		bring	brought	brought
buy	bought	bought		burst	burst	burst

Name the past and perfect form of:

Name the past and perfect form of:

CATCH

CHOOSE

Grammar Basics

Grammar Basics

Name the past and perfect form of:

Name the past and perfect form of:

CLING

COME

Grammar Basics

Grammar Basics

Name the past and perfect form of:

Name the past and perfect form of:

COST

CREEP

| choose | chose | chosen | | catch | caught | caught |

| come | came | come | | cling | clung | clung |

| creep | crept | crept | | cost | cost | cost |

Name the past and perfect form of:

Name the past and perfect form of:

DEAL

DIG

Grammar Basics

Grammar Basics

Name the past and perfect form of:

Name the past and perfect form of:

DIVE

DO

Grammar Basics

Grammar Basics

Name the past and perfect form of:

Name the past and perfect form of:

DRAW

DRINK

| dig | dug | dug | | deal | dealt | dealt |

| do | did | done | | dive | dived | dived |

| drink | drank | drunk | | draw | drew | drawn |

Name the past and perfect form of:

Name the past and perfect form of:

DRIVE

EAT

Grammar Basics

Grammar Basics

Name the past and perfect form of:

Name the past and perfect form of:

FALL

FIGHT

Grammar Basics

Grammar Basics

Name the past and perfect form of:

Name the past and perfect form of:

FIND

FLING

| eat | ate | eaten | | drive | drove | driven |

| fight | fought | fought | | fall | fell | fallen |

| fling | flung | flung | | find | found | found |

Grammar Basics

Name the past and perfect form of:

FLY

Grammar Basics

Name the past and perfect form of:

FREEZE

Grammar Basics

Name the past and perfect form of:

GET

Grammar Basics

Name the past and perfect form of:

GIVE

Grammar Basics

Name the past and perfect form of:

GO

Grammar Basics

Name the past and perfect form of:

GROW

| freeze | froze | frozen | | fly | flew | flown |

| give | gave | given | | get | got | gotten |

| grow | grew | grown | | go | went | gone |

Name the past and perfect form of:

HAVE

Name the past and perfect form of:

HEAR

Grammar Basics

Name the past and perfect form of:

KEEP

Grammar Basics

Name the past and perfect form of:

KNOW

Grammar Basics

Name the past and perfect form of:

LAY

Grammar Basics

Name the past and perfect form of:

LEAD

hear	heard	heard		have	had	had
know	knew	known		keep	kept	kept
lead	led	led		lay	laid	laid

Name the past and perfect form of:

LEND

Name the past and perfect form of:

LET

Name the past and perfect form of:

LIE (RECLINE)

Name the past and perfect form of:

LOSE

Name the past and perfect form of:

READ

Name the past and perfect form of:

RIDE

| let | let | let | | lend | lent | lent |

| lose | lost | lost | | lie | lay | lain |

| ride | rode | ridden | | read | read | read |

Name the past and perfect form of:

RING

Name the past and perfect form of:

RISE

Name the past and perfect form of:

RUN

Name the past and perfect form of:

SAY

Name the past and perfect form of:

SEE

Name the past and perfect form of:

SET (PLACE)

| rise | rose | risen | | ring | rang | rung |

| say | said | said | | run | ran | run |

| set | set | set | | see | saw | seen |

Name the past and perfect form of:

Name the past and perfect form of:

SHAKE

SING

Grammar Basics

Grammar Basics

Name the past and perfect form of:

Name the past and perfect form of:

SINK

SIT

Grammar Basics

Grammar Basics

Name the past and perfect form of:

Name the past and perfect form of:

SPEAK

SPIN

| sing | sang | sung | | shake | shook | shaken |

| sit | sat | sat | | sink | sank | sunk |

| spin | spun | spun | | speak | spoke | spoken |

Name the past and perfect form of:

SPRING

Name the past and perfect form of:

STEAL

Name the past and perfect form of:

STING

Name the past and perfect form of:

SWEAR

Name the past and perfect form of:

SWIM

Name the past and perfect form of:

SWING

steal   stole   stolen   spring   sprang   sprung

swear   swore   sworn   sting   stung   stung

swing   swung   swung   swim   swam   swum

Name the past and perfect form of:

TAKE

Name the past and perfect form of:

TEACH

Grammar Basics

Name the past and perfect form of:

TEAR

Grammar Basics

Name the past and perfect form of:

THROW

Grammar Basics

Name the past and perfect form of:

WEAR

Grammar Basics

Name the past and perfect form of:

WRITE

teach	taught	taught		take	took	taken

throw	threw	thrown		tear	tore	torn

write	wrote	written		wear	wore	worn

Grammar Basics

Which is the right preposition?

He was absent *from/in* class three times last week.

Grammar Basics

Which is the right preposition?

The President accused his opponent *as/of* lying about the event.

Grammar Basics

Which is the right preposition?

Consuelo was accustomed *of/to* taking tea at 4:00 P.M.

Grammar Basics

Which is the right preposition?

The teacher was very well acquainted *about/with* the new subject matter on the test.

Grammar Basics

Which is the right preposition?

I'm not afraid *of/to* public speaking.

Grammar Basics

Which is the right preposition?

Jovan was very annoyed *on/with* the salesperson who sold him that computer.

The correct idiom is "accused of."

The correct idiom is "absent from."

The correct idiom is "acquainted with."

The correct idiom is "accustomed to."

The correct idiom is "annoyed with."

The correct idiom is "afraid of."

Grammar Basics

Which is the right preposition?

He apologized *about/for* the tone of his words, but not the content.

Grammar Basics

Which is the right preposition?

These errors arise *by/from* carelessness.

Grammar Basics

Which is the right preposition?

I prefer modern designs *as/of* a whole.

Grammar Basics

Which is the right preposition?

These symptoms are associated *to/with* the common cold.

Grammar Basics

Which is the right preposition?

I am aware *about/of* these issues because I read the newspaper.

Grammar Basics

Which is the right preposition?

She shouldn't make her decision on the basis *by/of* just one opinion.

The correct idiom is "arise from."

The correct idiom is "apologized for."

The correct idiom is "associated with."

The correct idiom is "as a whole."

The correct idiom is "basis of."

The correct idiom is "aware of."

Grammar Basics

Which is the right preposition?

Although I believe *about/in* extraterrestrial life, I'm skeptical about most UFO sightings.

Grammar Basics

Which is the right preposition?

She belongs *into/to* four clubs, tutors math, and still finds time to ski.

Grammar Basics

Which is the right preposition?

Although he himself broke it, Joe blamed his brother *about/for* the broken vase.

Grammar Basics

Which is the right preposition?

Personal computers first came *in/into* use in the 1980s.

Grammar Basics

Which is the right preposition?

Most people are capable *of/to* great things with a little encouragement.

Grammar Basics

Which is the right preposition?

Our band is committed *with/to* giving six performances at that club.

The correct idiom is " belongs to."

The correct idiom is "believe in."

The correct idiom is "came into use."

The correct idiom is "blamed for."

The correct idiom is "committed to."

The correct idiom is "capable of."

Grammar Basics

Which is the right preposition?

Water is composed *of/with* hydrogen and oxygen.

Grammar Basics

Which is the right preposition?

The concept *about/of* time travel is taken seriously only in science fiction.

Grammar Basics

Which is the right preposition?

The office worker was concerned *about/on* how the transit strike would affect her commute.

Grammar Basics

Which is the right preposition?

Alicia no longer seemed confused *about/over* the test directions.

Grammar Basics

Which is the right preposition?

The bones are connected *to/with* one another by ligaments.

Grammar Basics

Which is the right preposition?

Slava was not conscious *about/of* her slip of the tongue.

The correct idiom is "concept of."

The correct idiom is "composed of."

The correct idiom is "confused about."

The correct idiom is "concerned about."

The correct idiom is "conscious of."

The correct idiom is "connected to."

Grammar Basics

Which is the right preposition?

The new coach contributes *by/to* an exciting team spirit.

Grammar Basics

Which is the right preposition?

Her head was covered *on/with* snowflakes after sledding.

Grammar Basics

Which is the right preposition?

The agency is dedicated *about/to* child welfare.

Grammar Basics

Which is the right preposition?

There is no difference *among/between* the two brands of juice.

Grammar Basics

Which is the right preposition?

The oxygen-poor blood in a vein is very different *between/from* the oxygen-rich blood in an artery.

Grammar Basics

Which is the right preposition?

This species is distinguished *between/from* the other lizards by its large orange spots.

The correct idiom is "covered with."

The correct idiom is "contributes to."

The correct idiom is "difference between."

The correct idiom is "dedicated to."

The correct idiom is "distinguish between."

The correct idiom is "different from."

Grammar Basics

Which is the right preposition?

"Never again!" Ali declared. "I'm done *by/with* last-minutc studying."

Grammar Basics

Which is the right preposition?

Pyoter was encouraged *by/for* the teacher's praise of his poem.

Grammar Basics

Which is the right preposition?

Yolanda escaped *into/from* the boring lecture, giggling as she made her excuses.

Grammar Basics

Which is the right preposition?

Leonardo da Vinci excelled *about/in* science and engineering, as well as the arts.

Grammar Basics

Which Is the right preposition?

"World peace and freedom are still worth fighting *with/for*," concluded the politician.

Grammar Basics

Which is thc right preposition?

"I thought you were finished *for/with* your history paper," Shantal exclaimed to Cheryl.

The correct idiom is "encouraged by."

The correct idiom is "done with."

The correct idiom is "excelled in."

The correct idiom is "escaped from."

The correct idiom is "finished with."

The correct idiom is "fighting for." We "fight with" our enemies, but "for" our goals.

Grammar Basics

Which is the right preposition?

Joshua was so fond *of/on* chocolate chip cookies that he ate them for breakfast!

Grammar Basics

Which is the right preposition?

The kids raised a great deal *in/of* money for cancer just by selling lemonade.

Grammar Basics

Which is the right preposition?

The growth *in/of* the economy in one sector failed to make up for the losses in the other.

Grammar Basics

Which is the right preposition?

She may be thoughtless, but she's not guilty *from/of* deliberately hurting anyone.

Grammar Basics

Which is the right preposition?

I hid the comic books *against/from* my kid brother, but he found them anyway.

Grammar Basics

Which is the right preposition?

She was hinting *for/at* borrowing my green shoes, but I just ignored her.

The correct idiom is "great deal of."

The correct idiom is "fond of."

The correct idiom is "guilty of."

The correct idiom is "growth of."

The correct idiom is "hint at." We "ask for" but "hint at" what we want.

The correct idiom is "hide from."

Grammar Basics

Which is the right preposition?

He gave me a B–, but I really hoped *for/to* something better.

Grammar Basics

Which is the right preposition?

"The administration has no right to impose a dress code *at/on* us," exclaimed Roberto, the student president.

Grammar Basics

Which is the right preposition?

I first heard the professor's name in connection *to/with* the engineering society.

Grammar Basics

Which is the right preposition?

The senior showed an indifference *for/to* his career that troubled his parents.

Grammar Basics

Which is the right preposition?

My sister insists *for/on* cleanliness and order in her room, but my brother is a slob.

Grammar Basics

Which is the right preposition?

Medina was instrumental *for/in* creating a peer counseling service at school.

The correct idiom is "impose on."

The correct idiom is "hoped for."

The correct idiom is "indifference to."

The correct idiom is "in connection with."

The correct idiom is "instrumental in."

The correct idiom is "insist on."

Which is the right preposition?

Quarla was interested *about/in* anatomy in sophomore year.

Which is the right preposition?

"Should you really be involved *for/in* seven clubs?" Chien asked her exhausted sister.

Which is the right preposition?

The teacher's habit of cracking her knuckles was irritating *to/with* the class.

Which is the right preposition?

The college was known *about/for* its elite journalism programs.

Which is the right preposition?

The publication of that first story led *on/to* a fulfilling career as a writer.

Which is the right preposition?

The solution, the scientist found, lay *by/in* the simplest formula of all.

The correct idiom is "involved in."

The correct idiom is "interested in."

The correct idiom is "known for."

The correct idiom is "irritating to."

The correct idiom is "lie in." The past tense of "lie" is "lay."

The correct idiom is "lead to." The past tense of "lead" is "led."

Grammar Basics

Which is the right preposition?

The goals of that clique are limited *between/to* fashion and dating.

Grammar Basics

Which is the right preposition?

Complete honesty is necessary *to/as* a good relationship.

Grammar Basics

Which is the right preposition?

The lawyer objected *from/to* the motion vigorously

Grammar Basics

Which is the right preposition?

The clerk obtained the files *from/at* the department head just before the 5:00 deadline.

Grammar Basics

Which is the right preposition?

Ira was opposed *at/to* the idea of a revolt from the day it was suggested.

Grammar Basics

Which is the right preposition?

High school students should participate *between/in* extracurricular activities.

The correct idiom is "necessary to."

The correct idiom is "limited to."

The correct idiom is "obtain from."

The correct idiom is "objected to."

The correct idiom is "participate in."

The correct idiom is "opposed to."

Grammar Basics

Which is the right preposition?

Carmen was pleased *of/with* her top score on the test.

Grammar Basics

Which is the right preposition?

The students were posing *for/to* their yearbook photos all Tuesday.

Grammar Basics

Which is the right preposition?

The commissioner wasn't prepared *by/for* the journalist's trick question.

Grammar Basics

Which is the right preposition?

I couldn't prevent him *from/with* going into that cold water.

Grammar Basics

Which is the right preposition?

Albert Einstein was proclaimed *as/for* a genius only in later life.

Grammar Basics

Which is the right preposition?

Women were prohibited *for/from* voting until 1922.

The correct idiom is "posing for."

The correct idiom is "pleased with."

The correct idiom is "prevent from."

The correct idiom is "prepared for."

The correct idiom is "prohibited from."

The correct idiom is "proclaimed as."

Grammar Basics

Which is the right preposition?

The faculty protested *against/in* the school's new budget cuts.

Grammar Basics

Which is the right preposition?

The whole town was proud *of/to* the soccer team's come-from-behind victory.

Grammar Basics

Which is the right preposition?

The environmentalists reacted *about/against* the proposal to develop the wilderness areas.

Grammar Basics

Which is the right preposition?

The inhabitants barely recovered *by/from* one storm only to be hit by another.

Grammar Basics

Which is the right preposition?

The recent fossil finds are closely related *to/with* fossils found one thousand miles away.

Grammar Basics

Which is the right preposition?

Thanks to the arrival of the helicopter, everyone was rescued *from/to* the fire.

The correct idiom is "proud of."

The correct idiom is "protest against."

The correct idiom is "recovered from."

The correct idiom is "reacted against."

The correct idiom is "rescued from."

The correct idiom is "related to."

Grammar Basics

Which is the right preposition?

The teacher responded *for/to* the question with another question.

Grammar Basics

Which is the right preposition?

Everyone here is responsible *for/from* keeping our work place clean.

Grammar Basics

Which is the right preposition?

That mix of chemicals will result *in/into* an explosion.

Grammar Basics

Which is the right preposition?

The judicial ruling was a reversal *of/on* the previous, unfair statute.

Grammar Basics

Which is the right preposition?

Sinead's tact made sure that everyone was satisfied *by/with* the seating arrangement.

Grammar Basics

Which is the right preposition?

The scene *from/of* the robbery was off limits to everyone except the detectives.

The correct idiom is "responsible for."

The correct idiom is "responded to."

The correct idiom is "reversal of."

The correct idiom is "result in"

The correct idiom is "scene of."

The correct idiom is "satisfied with."

Grammar Basics

Which is the right preposition?

The Belgian Shepherd is similar *among/to* other shepherd dogs except for its smaller size.

Grammar Basics

Which is the right preposition?

It's not polite to stare *at/by* people.

Grammar Basics

Which is the right preposition?

The doctor suggested knitting to stop me *from/of* biting my nails.

Grammar Basics

Which is the right preposition?

A few crackers are no substitute *for/of* a well-balanced meal.

Grammar Basics

Which is the right preposition?

With hard work and positive thinking, you can succeed *in/with* everything you do.

Grammar Basics

Which is the right preposition?

The poor gardener suffered *from/with* hay fever every spring.

The correct idiom is "stare at."

The correct idiom is "similar to."

The correct idiom is "substitute for."

The correct idiom is "stop from."

The correct idiom is "suffered from."

The correct idiom is "succeed in."

Grammar Basics

Which is the right preposition?

Everyone sympathized *for/with* Marta when her computer crashed.

Grammar Basics

Which is the right preposition?

I had my mother, a pianist, to thank *for/of* my musical ability.

Grammar Basics

Which is the right preposition?

It would have been wise to bring an umbrella, but we didn't think *of/to* it.

Grammar Basics

Which is the right preposition?

The children got tired *of/with* television and read their books instead.

Grammar Basics

Which is the right preposition?

Ardus didn't do well as a computer technician, but he triumphed *as/in* a teacher.

Grammar Basics

Which is the right preposition?

The mother was upset *about/with* her teenage son for coming home late.

The correct idiom is "thank for."

The correct idiom is "sympathize with."

The correct idiom is "tired of."

The correct idiom is "think of."

The correct idiom is "upset with."

The correct idiom is "triumph as."

Grammar Basics

Which is the right preposition?

Jimi is used *about/to* the long hours of practice needed to be a figure skater.

Grammar Basics

Which is the right preposition?

"Who did you vote *for/of* in the election?" the reporter asked the bystanders.

Grammar Basics

Which is the right preposition?

He went *about/with* saying that I didn't deserve the prize, which wasn't true.

Grammar Basics

Which is the right preposition?

The parties were willing *between/to* negotiate, so a settlement was reached.

Grammar Basics

Which is the right preposition?

With the help *by/of* my tutor, I got the third-highest math grade in my class.

Grammar Basics

Which is the right preposition?

The neighbors always worry too much *about/among* the appearance of their lawn.

The correct idiom is "vote for."

The correct idiom is "used to."

The correct idiom is "willing to."

The correct idiom is "went about."

The correct idiom is "worry about."

The correct idiom is "with the help of."

Grammar Basics

Complete the idiom correctly.

Brita is able *doing/to do* forty-seven push-ups without stopping.

Grammar Basics

Complete the idiom correctly.

Being so macho, he wouldn't admit *having/to having* cried at the movies.

Grammar Basics

Complete the idiom correctly.

I can't afford *missing/to miss* the class before the test.

Grammar Basics

Complete the idiom correctly.

Her mother would never allow her *going/to go* to the really good rap concerts.

Grammar Basics

Complete the idiom correctly.

Joel anticipated *meeting/to meet* the girl of his dreams at the skating rink tonight.

Grammar Basics

Complete the idiom correctly.

I'd appreciate your *taking/to take* the time to make the new kids feel welcome.

The correct idiom is "admit to having."

The correct idiom is "able to."

The correct idiom is "allow to go."

The correct idiom is "afford to miss."

The correct idiom is "appreciate your taking the time."

The correct idiom is "anticipated meeting."

Complete the idiom correctly.

The young man contemplated *joining/to join* the Army, but his parents objected.

Complete the idiom correctly.

If you continue *procrastinating/to procrastinate*, you will certainly flunk biology.

Complete the idiom correctly.

After the director yelled at him, the actor decided *quitting/to quit* the play.

Complete the idiom correctly.

Truman was allowed to defer *serving/to serve* on jury duty because of financial hardship.

Complete the idiom correctly.

You can't delay *seeing/to see* a doctor when you fracture a bone.

Complete the idiom correctly.

The jewel thief denied *stealing/to steal* the heirlooms.

The correct idiom is "continue to procrastinate."

The correct idiom is "contemplated joining."

The correct idiom is "defer serving."

The correct idiom is "decided to quit."

The correct idiom is "deny stealing."

The correct idiom is "delay seeing."

Grammar Basics

Complete the idiom correctly.

All the students in that class deserve *taking/to take* a day off from studying.

Grammar Basics

Complete the idiom correctly.

The new ingredient enables the medication to *work/working* faster.

Grammar Basics

Complete the idiom correctly.

The new literacy program encourages *reading/to read* at an early age.

Grammar Basics

Complete the idiom correctly.

Gladys enjoyed *playing/to play* backgammon and chess.

Grammar Basics

Complete the idiom correctly.

That hike entails *climbing/ to climb* a hundred-foot rock face.

Grammar Basics

Complete the idiom correctly.

The new teacher expects us *knowing/to know* these word lists by Tuesday.

The correct idiom is "enable to work."

The correct idiom is "deserve to take."

The correct idiom is "enjoyed playing."

The correct idiom is "encourage reading."

The correct idiom is "expects us to know."

The correct idiom is "entails climbing."

Grammar Basics

Complete the idiom correctly.

These audio tapes facilitate *learning/to learn* French.

Grammar Basics

Complete the idiom correctly.

The scuba diver failed *noticing/to notice* the barracuda just left of him.

Grammar Basics

Complete the idiom correctly.

Will she ever finish *painting/to paint* that mural?

Grammar Basics

Complete the idiom correctly.

Andrew had given up *hoping/to hope* he'd be accepted to college when he got into Yale.

Grammar Basics

Complete the idiom correctly.

The lifeguard didn't hesitate *jumping/to jump* in the water and rescue the crying boy.

Grammar Basics

Complete the idiom correctly.

I hope *practicing/to practice* medicine in my hometown one day.

The correct idiom is "fail to notice."

The correct idiom is "facilitate learning."

The correct idiom is "give up hoping."

The correct idiom is "finish painting."

The correct idiom is "hope to practice."

The correct idiom is "hesitate to jump."

Grammar Basics

Complete the idiom correctly.

Roger imagined *playing/to play* the bassoon to enthusiastic crowds.

Grammar Basics

Complete the idiom correctly.

The detective intended *luring/to lure* the criminal to the scene of the crime.

Grammar Basics

Complete the idiom correctly.

The job involves *to write/writing* the dialog for the show.

Grammar Basics

Complete the idiom correctly.

Although she may be a difficult person, nothing justifies *raising/to raise* your voice.

Grammar Basics

Complete the idiom correctly.

"Keep *going/to go*, you're almost there!" Houra cried as Sadie neared the finish line.

Grammar Basics

Complete the idiom correctly.

With these recipes, you can learn *liking/to like* all kinds of vegetables.

The correct idiom is "intend to lure."

The correct idiom is "imagine playing."

The correct idiom is "justifies raising."

The correct idiom is "involves writing."

The correct idiom is "learn to like."

The correct idiom is "keep going."

Grammar Basics

Complete the idiom correctly.

The seniors liked *going/to go* for a midnight swim after finals.

Grammar Basics

Complete the idiom correctly.

Hassan not only meant *to win/winning* the 400-yard dash, he intended to set a school record.

Grammar Basics

Complete the idiom correctly.

Hoping I would find them, I didn't mention *losing/to lose* the earrings to my sister.

Grammar Basics

Complete the idiom correctly.

The children missed *to visit/visiting* their grandparents in the country that summer.

Grammar Basics

Complete the idiom correctly.

Will this error necessitate our *redoing/to redo* the whole experiment?

Grammar Basics

Complete the idiom correctly.

The mad scientist neglected *including/to include* an off-switch for his monster.

The correct idiom is "mean to win."

The correct idiom is "like to go."

The correct idiom is "miss visiting."

The correct idiom is "mention losing."

The correct idiom is "neglect to include."

The correct idiom is "necessitate redoing."

Grammar Basics

Complete the idiom correctly.

Practice *pronouncing/to pronounce* the Spanish verbs in chapter four.

Grammar Basics

Complete the idiom correctly.

Angela preferred *making/to make* all her telephone calls while waiting for the bus.

Grammar Basics

Complete the idiom correctly.

I'm not prepared *giving/to give* up on learning calculus yet.

Grammar Basics

Complete the idiom correctly.

The case will prevent *scratching/to scratch* and other damage to your glasses.

Grammar Basics

Complete the idiom correctly.

The small boy pretended *being/to be* asleep when his mother looked in.

Grammar Basics

Complete the idiom correctly.

The way it's going, this song promises *being/to be* the number one hit in the nation soon.

The correct idiom is "prefer to make."

The correct idiom is "practice pronouncing."

The correct idiom is "prevent scratching."

The correct idiom is "prepare to give up."

The correct idiom is "promises to be."

The correct idiom is "pretended to be asleep."

Grammar Basics

Complete the idiom correctly.

The family threw a big party the day that Grandpa quit *smoking/to smoke.*

Grammar Basics

Complete the idiom correctly.

The locals recommended *driving/to drive* the longer but more scenic route.

Grammar Basics

Complete the idiom correctly.

I refuse *believing/to believe* that we can't increase the circulation of this newspaper.

Grammar Basics

Complete the idiom correctly.

The girls reported *seeing/to see* a red-tailed hawk nesting on the skyscraper.

Grammar Basics

Complete the idiom correctly.

Sheila never had to struggle *to understand/understanding* math.

Grammar Basics

Complete the idiom correctly.

The male black widow spider tends *being/to be* much smaller than the female.

The correct idiom is "recommended driving."

The correct idiom is "quit smoking."

The correct idiom is "reported seeing."

The correct idiom is "refuse to believe."

The correct idiom is "tends to be."

The correct idiom is "struggle to understand."

Complete the idiom correctly.

Since it was threatening *raining/to rain* again, Luz took her new pink umbrella.

Complete the idiom correctly.

They don't tolerate *cheating/to cheat* of any kind at that school.

Complete the idiom correctly.

I'd understand *going/to go* to the amusement park once, but twice?

Complete the idiom correctly.

Jolie urged me *buying/to buy* the lime green pants, and I'm so glad I did!

Complete the idiom correctly.

The twins volunteered *doing/to do* the dishes, one washing, one drying.

Complete the idiom correctly.

I want *learning/to learn* how to make horror movies in college

The correct idiom is "tolerate cheating."

The correct idiom is "threatening to rain."

The correct idiom is "urged me to buy."

The correct idiom is "understand going."

The correct idiom is "want to learn."

The correct idiom is "volunteered to do."

Word Choice

Choose the correct word.

We divided the candy *between/among* the three of us.

Word Choice

Choose the correct word.

The soloist performed *impressibly/impressively* at the concert, although she was far from well.

Word Choice

Choose the correct word.

The attendant was *unconscious/subconscious* of the dangerous situation she had created by leaving her cart in the aisle.

Word Choice

Choose the correct word.

Although the hurricane was *eminent/imminent*, the family refused to evacuate their home.

Word Choice

Choose the correct word.

The tennis player used an *underhand/underhanded* serve in practice to rest his injured shoulder.

Word Choice

Choose the correct word.

It was *imprudent/impudent* of the teacher to let the class leave early.

The correct word, *impressively*, means "in a manner likely to impress." The wrong choice, *impressibly*, means "in a manner that is easily influenced" and doesn't make sense.

The correct word is *among*. *Between* can only be used with two persons or items.

The correct word, *imminent*, means "very near and certain, impending." The wrong choice, *eminent*, means "distinguished, of high repute," as in "an eminent philosopher."

The correct word, *unconscious*, means "unaware." The wrong word, *subconscious*, means "not fully or wholly conscious," as in "a subconscious motive."

The correct word, *imprudent*, means "rash, indiscreet." The wrong choice, *impudent*, means "insolently disrespectful, presumptuous."

The correct word, *underhand* is used in the literal sense, swinging down instead of up.

Word Choice

Choose the correct word.

At the water park, my favorite ride is a long, straight *chute/shoot*.

Word Choice

Choose the correct word.

Ms. Kerwin tried to *elicit/solicit* a response to her questions about the book, but no one had read it.

Word Choice

Choose the correct word.

Dr. Lewis had us do an experiment to see whether the salt was *soluble/solvable* in water.

Word Choice

Choose the correct word.

The ship was *stationary/stationery*, having dropped its anchor.

Word Choice

Choose the correct word.

That sweater is perfect *compliment/complement* to your blue eyes.

Word Choice

Choose the correct word.

At work, we have *periodic/periodical* reviews to make sure everyone is on track.

The correct word, *solicit*, means "to request a response," while the wrong choice, *elicit*, means "to get a response."

The correct choice, *chute*, means "an inclined channel or passage."

The correct choice is *stationary*, meaning "immobile." The wrong word, *stationery*, refers to writing paper.

Soluble, the correct word, means "dissolvable." The wrong choice, *solvable*, means "having a solution or answer."

Periodic is the correct word, meaning "occurring at regular intervals." The wrong word, *periodical*, means "published at regular intervals."

The correct word is *complement*, which means "an adequate supplement." The wrong word, *compliment*, is "a laudatory remark."

Word Choice

Choose the correct word.

Minority populations have been *prosecuted/persecuted* by the majority many times in history.

Word Choice

Choose the correct word.

After Kevin had left the stage, Marcus *preceded/proceeded* to collect his diploma next.

Word Choice

Choose the correct word.

Ms. Carpenter had to send three students to the *principal's/principle's* office after a fight broke out in the hall.

Word Choice

Choose the correct word.

When Nathan said his headaches were not improving, the doctor *proscribed/prescribed* a stronger medication.

Word Choice

Choose the correct word.

The lawyer strode *purposefully/purposely* into the courtroom to give the jury the impression that he was confident.

Word Choice

Choose the correct word.

In a *navel/naval* dispute, it is not always the side with the most ships that wins.

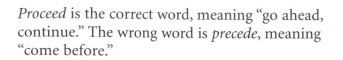

Proceed is the correct word, meaning "go ahead, continue." The wrong word is *precede*, meaning "come before."

The correct word is *persecute*, which means "oppress." *Prosecute*, the wrong choice, means "bring legal action against."

Prescribe means "impose authoritatively," and is the correct word. *Proscribe* means "prohibit," and is the wrong word in this context.

The correct word here is *principal*, which means "the head of a school," while the wrong choice, *principle*, means "primary."

Naval, meaning "relating to the navy" is correct in this context, not *navel*, meaning "belly-button."

The correct word is *purposefully*, which means "with a specific purpose." The wrong word is *purposely*, which means "on purpose, deliberately."

Word Choice

Choose the correct word.

We brought everything we needed for the camping trip, *accept/except* my brother forgot his sleeping bag.

Word Choice

Choose the correct word.

Most college dormitories allow *excess/access* to the buildings only to those who live there.

Word Choice

Choose the correct word.

Animals raised in captivity are often unable to *adapt/adopt* to life in the wild.

Word Choice

Choose the correct word.

Marcy wondered what *effect/affect* her improved SAT score would have on her college admissions prospects.

Word Choice

Choose the correct word.

Luke's dog showed her *affectation/affection* for him by wagging her tail and licking his face.

Word Choice

Choose the correct word.

Often during a political debate, candidates will illustrate their positions with a pertinent *anecdote/antidote*.

Access, meaning "right of entry" is the correct choice, while *excess* means "too much."

The correct word is *except*, which means "not including." *Accept* means "to receive."

Affect and *effect* are easy to confuse, since their meanings are related. However, *effect,* the correct choice here, is a noun meaning "a result or consequence," and *affect* is a verb meaning "to have a result or consequence."

The correct choice is *adapt*, which means "adjust to." *Adopt* means "to take on."

An *anecdote* is "a personal story," making it the best choice for this sentence. An *antidote* is "a remedy given the counteract poison or illness."

An *affectation* is "a mannerism or quirk," whereas *affection*, the correct answer, means "fondness."

Word Choice

Choose the correct word.

The editor's harsh and unhelpful *critique/criticism* of the manuscript devastated the insecure writer.

Word Choice

Choose the correct word.

Many people thought that today's youth were *apathetic/empathetic* until they heard about the widespread demonstrations on college campuses.

Word Choice

Choose the correct word.

Although Julia was not a morning person, she found it easy to *arise/arouse* early while she was traveling in Europe.

Word Choice

Choose the correct word.

The unadorned walls and simple furniture in the monastery attested to the *aesthetic/ascetic* principles of the monks who lived there.

Word Choice

Choose the correct word.

Although the school administration did not agree with all the opinions voiced in the student newspaper, in the interest of free speech they chose not to *censor/censure* the publication.

Word Choice

Choose the correct word.

Several billionaires have attempted *circumlocution/circumnavigation* of the globe in hot air balloons.

Apathetic, meaning "not caring" is the correct choice here, rather than *empathetic*, which means "compassionate."

The best word here is *criticism* since it was negative and unhelpful; *critique* means "analysis."

Ascetic means "austere," making it the best choice here. *Aesthetic* means "concerned with beauty."

The correct word is *arise*, which means "get up," rather than *arouse* which means "stimulate."

The correct word, *circumnavigation*, means "to go around the earth," while *circumlocution* means "wordy."

Censor is the correct word in this sentence. It means "to repress." *Censure* means "to reprimand."

Choose the correct word.

Choose the correct word.

The principal felt she should not *condone/condole* the disruptive behavior of the students on the field trip so she suspended them.

Sarah was *contemptuous/contemptible* of anyone who did poorly in school, which did not make her a popular student.

Choose the correct word.

Choose the correct word.

Although Marissa is a vegetarian for moral reasons, she refuses to see the *contraction/contradiction* in wearing a leather jacket.

The muffler of the car was so badly *corrosive/corroded* that it was in danger of falling off.

Choose the correct word.

Choose the correct word.

Liz has ridden horses since she was a small girl, and she is now quite *crafty/skillful* at jumps.

Jack's father did not find his son's excuse for missing curfew *credible/credulous*, so Jack was grounded.

Contemptuous, the correct choice, means "disdainful or condescending." *Contemptible* means "disgraceful."

The correct word, *condone*, means "overlook or excuse," while the incorrect word, *condole*, means "comfort"

The right word is *corroded*, which means "rotten," rather than *corrosive*, which means "causing corrosion."

Contradiction is the correct word here, meaning "inconsistency." *Contraction* means "tighten."

Credible, the right choice, means "believable." *Credulous* means "gullible."

The word *crafty* means "cunning" and implies deviousness. The better choice here is *skillful*.

Word Choice

Choose the correct word.

The measure passed in the city council by *anonymous/unanimous* vote: the only member who might have dissented was not present that day.

Word Choice

Choose the correct word.

In the nineteenth century, it was not considered *decorous/decorated* for women's ankles to show beneath their skirts.

Word Choice

Choose the correct word.

The head of the English department was delighted to hire Professor Cummings, whose book on Shakespeare's characters is considered the *definite/definitive* work on that subject.

Word Choice

Choose the correct word.

Although the math problem appeared to be very difficult, Matthew was able to *deride/derive* the answer quite easily.

Word Choice

Choose the correct word.

Although he was well over six feet tall, Greg was able to endure the *discomfort/discomfit* of flying in coach because he was so excited about the trip.

Word Choice

Choose the correct word.

Ms. Green knew that Sam was intelligent, so she felt his poor grades indicated that he was *disinterested/uninterested* in science.

Decorous, which means "proper," is the correct choice, rather than *decorated,* meaning "ornamented."

This one's a little tricky, since both words could be used to describe a vote. In this context, however, *unanimous*, meaning "everyone agreeing," is more appropriate than *anonymous*, which means "nameless."

Derive means "to obtain," and is the best choice here. *Deride* means "to make fun of."

The correct word is *definitive*, meaning "ultimate." *Definite* means "sure."

The best choice in this context is *uninterested*, which means "not interested." *Disinterested* means "unbiased."

The correct choice is *discomfort*, which means "uncomfortable." *Discomfit* means "humiliate."

Word Choice

Choose the correct word.

Kristin was dissatisfied with the *epilogue/epitaph* of the book; it tied up the loose ends a little too neatly.

Word Choice

Choose the correct word.

"Please *disregard/disrepute* my cats," Mrs. Stone told her guests, although Ann counted seven of them running around her ankles.

Word Choice

Choose the correct word.

After high school, the twins took *divergent/divisive* paths, as Allison went straight to college while Jennifer took a year to travel and study Spanish.

Word Choice

Choose the correct word.

Chris was quite *empathetic/emphatic* in telling his parents why he was responsible enough to take the car to the dance, and in the end he won them over.

Word Choice

Choose the correct word.

Mr. Lewis knew some of his students got drowsy in Calculus, so he tried to *enervate/energize* them by leading a round of jumping jacks in the middle of class.

Word Choice

Choose the correct word.

It is traditional for a close friend or relative to deliver an *elegy/eulogy* praising the deceased at a funeral.

Disregard, meaning "ignore" is a better choice in this context than *disrepute*, which means "having a bad reputation."

The word *epilogue* refers to "a chapter at the end of a book that sometimes will reveal the fate of its characters," and is the better choice here. An *epitaph* is "a memorializing inscription on a tombstone."

The right word is *emphatic*, which means "forceful." *Empathetic* means "compassionate."

The correct choice is *divergent*, meaning "different." *Divisive* means "discordant."

These two words are close in their meanings; however *eulogy*, "a speech given at a funeral," is more appropriate here. An *elegy* is "a song or poem of mourning."

Enervate means "to weaken," which is the opposite of the correct choice, *energize*.

Choose the correct word.

Although she had studied it in school, Lisa could not appreciate the *enmity/enormity* of geologic time until she visited the Grand Canyon.

Choose the correct word.

Until he studied organic farming, Michael did not realize that most fruit is *eradicated/irradiated* to slow the ripening process.

Choose the correct word.

Because of his strict upbringing, Tyrone knew that cheating on the test was not an *ethical/ethnic* thing to do.

Choose the correct word.

To avoid any *duplicity/duplication*, Mrs. Lang had each student write down what he or she planned to bring to the potluck.

Choose the correct word.

Maria *alluded/eluded* to that fact that she had met Jose before, but she was shy about revealing any details.

Choose the correct word.

After numerous attempts to put the tricycle together on Christmas Eve, Jim had to *dissemble/disassemble* the whole thing and start over when he found the missing part.

Irradiated, meaning "exposed to radiation," is the right word, whereas *eradicated* means "gotten rid of."

The correct word to choose here is *enormity*, meaning "hugeness." *Enmity* means "hostility."

Duplication is the right choice, meaning "repetition," while *duplicity* means "deception."

Ethical is the correct choice, meaning "moral or right." *Ethnic* means "racial or cultural."

Disassemble means "to take apart," and is the correct word choice here. *Dissemble* means "to evade."

Alluded means "made reference to, or suggested," making it the correct choice. *Eluded* means "got away, escaped."

Word Choice

Choose the correct word.

Looking at the menu, Chuck felt *indecisive/undetermined*: was he in the mood for salad or pasta?

Word Choice

Choose the correct word.

Rather than directly answer the reporter's question about the scandal, the politician *evaded/invaded* the issue by changing the subject.

Word Choice

Choose the correct word.

Although Olivia was a patient woman, her twin toddlers had the ability to *exacerbate/exasperate* her eventually.

Word Choice

Choose the correct word.

The school board tried to pass a comprehensive dress code for the whole district, but the members could not agree on what constituted *appropriate/expropriate* attire.

Word Choice

Choose the correct word.

Although Jessica and Victor had been dating for months, she insisted that he ask her *formally/formerly* to every high school dance.

Word Choice

Choose the correct word.

Mrs. Chang held her tongue as the decorator described his *grandiose/grand* plans for her dining room, but she made a mental note not to hire him.

Evaded is the right word here; it means "avoided." *Invaded* means "occupied by force."

Indecisive, meaning "unable to make up one's mind," is a better choice than *undetermined*, meaning "not yet decided."

Appropriate is the correct choice, "meaning suitable or proper," while *expropriate* means "to confiscate."

The correct choice here is *exasperate*, which means "frustrate, annoy." *Exacerbate* means "to make worse."

Grandiose, which means "ostentatious, excessively grand," is probably intended, since Mrs. Chang feels negative about the plans.

Formally is the correct word. It means "officially or in a formal manner." *Formerly* means "in the past, previously."

Word Choice

Choose the correct word.

When Gretchen was ten she chose wallpaper with a *floral/florid* pattern for her room, but by her teenage years she wanted something more edgy.

Word Choice

Choose the correct word.

After working in a restaurant, Ian became a better tipper because he knew waiters depend on these *gratuities/gratitudes*.

Word Choice

Choose the correct word.

Though Marcus was upset to see his ex-girlfriend flirting at the dance, his expression remained *impassable/impassive*.

Word Choice

Choose the correct word.

After a few days in jail, the suspect was ready to *imply/implicate* his accomplices in exchange for his own early release.

Word Choice

Choose the correct word.

Jordan is a very handy around the house; she even *instilled/installed* a new faucet in the bathroom.

Word Choice

Choose the correct word.

After hours of contract negotiations, neither side would budge and the issue remained *irresolute/unresolved* until the next meeting.

Gratuity means "extra, bonus" and is the correct choice. *Gratitude* means "thankfulness."

The best choice is *floral*, "having to do with flowers." *Florid* means "elaborate and ornate."

The right word is *implicate*, meaning "incriminate." *Imply* means "suggest."

Impassive is the correct word; it means "unemotional, blank." *Impassable* means "blocked."

Unresolved means "not settled, up in the air." It is the correct choice. *Irresolute* means "unsure."

The correct choice, *install*, meaning "to set up," usually applies to things, while *instill*, meaning "to impress ideas upon," usually applies to people.

Word Choice

Choose the correct word.

After a long day on his feet, Max likes to *lie/lay* down for a few minutes when he gets home from work.

Word Choice

Choose the correct word.

In the frontier days of the American West, whole communities would come together to help *rise/raise* a barn for one family.

Word Choice

Choose the correct word.

After a long summer at camp, Lane was *loathe/loath* to go back to school.

Word Choice

Choose the correct word.

Jerry did not approve of the way his friend Lydia *malingered/maligned* her boss.

Word Choice

Choose the correct word.

When she sat down to take the test, Vu had a *momentous/momentary* feeling of panic, but it passed when she remember how well she had prepared.

Word Choice

Choose the correct word.

Margo's friends worried that she would be *morose/morass* after the break-up with Nick.

These words are very similar in meaning, but the correct choice is *raise*, "to cause to rise to a standing position." *Rise* itself means "to assume a standing position."

The two words are often confused. *Lie* means "to recline" and is correct in this context. *Lay* means "to put or place."

Malign means "to slander" and is correct. *Malinger* means "to feign illness."

Loath, an adjective meaning "unwilling, reluctant," is correct. The incorrect word, *loathe*, is a verb meaning "to hate"

The right word is *morose*, which means "depressed or gloomy." A *morass* is " a big mess."

The correct choice is *momentary*, meaning "brief, fleeting," while *momentous* means "significant."

Word Choice

Choose the correct word.

When Kali went through a goth phase, black became the *predominant/predominate* color in her wardrobe.

Word Choice

Choose the correct word.

Stephen King is a very *proliferate/prolific* author, turning out many books each year.

Word Choice

Choose the correct word.

I couldn't recall the *amount/number* of times I had already explained the process to her.

Word Choice

Choose the correct word.

In a crisis, sometimes a *reactive/reactionary* measure is the best solution.

Word Choice

Choose the correct word.

"You are *resplendent/splendid*," said Anthony to his prom date, whose sparkly dress caught the lights on the dance floor.

Word Choice

Choose the correct word.

Celebrities sometimes win a *liable/libel* suit against the tabloids if it is proven that a story was a fabrication.

Prolific, meaning "productive," is the right word. The wrong choice, *proliferate*, means "to reproduce."

Predominant means "main, major," and makes the most sense here. *Predominate* means "to prevail."

Reactive, which means "reacting to events as they occur," is a better fit than *reactionary*, meaning "opposed to political change, conservative."

Amount is used when we can't count the items; *number* is used when we can.

Libel means "a written or oral defamation" and is the correct choice. *Liable* means "responsible."

Splendid, meaning "excellent," is not as good a choice here as the correct word, *resplendent*, meaning "having a dazzling appearance."

Word Choice

Choose the correct word.

There were *fewer/less* marbles in the bag than we expected, so some must have been lost.

Word Choice

Choose the correct word.

"Come and *sit/set* next to me," my grandmother always says when I go visit her.

Word Choice

Choose the correct word.

David wondered if Karen's reasons for wanting to study at his house might be *specious/special*, since she always lost interest in Biology when his brother came home.

Word Choice

Choose the correct word.

Having grown up in a small town, Becca was not used to the *urban/urbane* sprawl she encountered when she moved to Los Angeles.

Word Choice

Choose the correct word.

This is the novel *in which/where* the young boy is kidnapped and is rescued by the Scottish outlaw.

Word Choice

Choose the correct word.

The *ostensible/ostentatious* reason for Gabrielle's visit was to welcome the new family to the neighborhood, but she really just wanted to see how they had decorated the house.

These words are closely related, but the correct choice is *sit*. *Set* means "to place."

When the objects compared can be counted, we use *fewer*. *Less* is used when objects can't be counted.

Urban, which means "relating to the city," is the correct choice. *Urbane* means "suave."

Specious means "false" and is the correct choice. *Special* means "extraordinary."

The correct word to choose here is *ostensible*, which means "supposed." *Ostentatious* means "showy or elaborate."

In which is the correct choice. *Where* should only be used to refer to physical location.

Instructions:

Each of these cards includes a sentence that contains one, and only one, error. See if you can identify the error, then check the explanation on the back to see how you did. Each explanation points out a second SAT issue that is correctly handled in the sentence, as well. All the issues that will be tested on the SAT are covered (see the reverse for a list).

I was so tired from climbing the hill, I couldn't hardly get over the fence.

Suddenly we realized that the boat, along with the crew and all our cargo, were sinking.

Last week, we are going to meet the class officers to discuss redecorating the cafeteria.

Last month he had earned his black belt.

Among you, Harry, and I, we earned over forty dollars washing windows today.

I was so tired from climbing the hill, I couldn't hardly get over the fence.

Idiom

Because the adverb "hardly" is a negative, the "not" in "couldn't" is an idiomatically incorrect double negative. The preposition "from" (in the first part of the sentence) is idiomatically correct.

The SAT commonly tested errors:
- Pronoun agreement
- Verb tenses
- Parallel
- Idiom
- Diction
- Run-ons and fragments
- Transitions
- Modifiers
- Wordiness
- Comparisons
- Irregular verbs
- Unnecessary passive
- Subject-verb agreement
- Ambiguity
- Adjective/adverb
- Noun agreement
- Comparative/superlative
- Pronoun case

Last week, we are going to meet the class officers to discuss redecorating the cafeteria.

Verb tense

"Last week" tells us the action is in the past; "we are going to meet" is illogically in the future. This might be corrected by changing "Last week" to "next week" or by using the past tense ("we met"). The phrase "to discuss" is idiomatically correct.

Suddenly we realized that the boat, along with the crew and all our cargo, were sinking.

Subject-verb agreement

The "boat" is the subject of the second clause; the crew and cargo are only part of an intervening phrase, so the verb should be "was"—not "were"—sinking. The prepositions "along with" are used correctly.

Among you, Harry, and I, we earned over forty dollars washing windows today.

Pronoun case

The list "you, Harry, and I" is not the subject here ("we" is); it is the object of the preposition "Among." So "I" should be "me." "Among" is correct diction, since more than two items are involved, but it may sound strange to you because most people say "between" in conversation.

Last month he had earned his black belt.

Verb tense

Standing by itself, this sentence can't be right on the SAT. It offers no explanation for using the perfect past tense, so the simple past should be used: "he earned." The phrase "earned his black belt" is idiomatically correct.

He put on his coat, boots, and hat, he would never again risk getting so cold in the Arctic air.

She never told her brother, but Anya felt very excited about him being nominated for the prize.

To win the prize, submit an essay telling us in 200 words or less how you would solve the overcrowding problem.

If you bring a guest along to the pool, be sure they wear their identification tag.

Pablo was grateful with his parents for their support and encouragement while he wrote the play.

Either of us have a better singing voice than that soprano.

She never told her brother, but Anya felt very excited about him being nominated for the prize.

Pronoun case

The correct phrase is "about his being nominated." The gerund takes the possessive form of the pronoun. The pronoun "him" (or "his") is not ambiguous here; it can only refer to Anya's brother; likewise, "She" and "her" can only refer to Anya.

He put on his coat, boots, and hat, he would never again risk getting so cold in the Arctic air.

Run-ons and fragments

There are two complete thoughts here, each with a subject and verb; therefore, this sentence needs a conjunction like "because" or a semicolon. The phrase "risk getting" is idiomatically correct.

If you bring a guest along to the pool, be sure they wear their identification tag.

Pronoun agreement

The pronouns "they" and "their" don't agree with their antecedent ("a guest"). Note that the sentence contains a hint: "identification tag" is singular, too. The phrase "bring…along" is idiomatically correct.

To win the prize, submit an essay telling us in 200 words or less how you would solve the overcrowding problem.

Idiom

When the items numbered are countable (as "words" are) the correct form is "fewer" rather than "less." This is an error you'll find in common use, but it's wrong on the SAT. The pronoun "us" is the correct case: you wouldn't say "tell we."

Either of us have a better singing voice than that soprano.

Subject-verb agreement

Not the pronoun ("us"), but "either" is the subject of this sentence. The verb should be singular ("has"). The idiom "better…than" is used correctly here.

Pablo was grateful with his parents for their support and encouragement while he wrote the play.

Idiom

The word "grateful" requires "to"—not "with"—in this context. The other phrases—"for their support" and "while he wrote"—are used correctly.

DNA fingerprinting, in conjunction with a growing database of similar crimes, serve as our most reliable evidence in this case.

Because Sal and Jo would be too far away to come home at noon, each of them brought lunches to the game.

After Amjed finished work, Alice, Sal, and him went to the game together.

The student's final thesis was not only well organized and carefully researched.

Just last week, in the first elections held since the fall of the tyrant, my 85-year-old great grandfather has cast his first vote in over 50 years.

Running all the way, refusing to stop even when she dropped her glove, without any thought for her aching feet.

Because Sal and Jo would be too far away to come home at noon, each of them brought lunches to the game.

Noun agreement

"Each" is singular, so each would have one lunch: "each of them brought lunch to the game." The phrase "of them" is not the subject (and if it were the subject, it would have to be in the subjective case, "they"). The structure "too … to …" is idiomatically correct.

DNA fingerprinting, in conjunction with a growing database of similar crimes, serve as our most reliable evidence in this case.

Subject-verb agreement

The subject is just "DNA fingerprinting"—not DNA fingerprinting and the database." Only "and" can create a compound (therefore plural) subject. So the verb should be singular, "serves." "Most reliable" is correct, since many types of evidence are compared.

The student's final thesis was not only well organized and carefully researched.

Idiom

The words "not only" require that the rest of the parallel structure be introduced by "but also" rather than "and." This kind of error is most common when you write too quickly, changing the structure of your sentence in mid-stream. That's one reason why proofreading your essay is vital.

After Amjed finished work, Alice, Sal, and him went to the game together.

Pronoun case

In this sentence, "Alice, Sal, and him" is the subject, and "him" should be "he." If a compound subject confuses you, try the pronoun alone as the subject: "him went to the game" makes it easier to see the error.

Running all the way, refusing to stop even when she dropped her glove, without any thought for her aching feet.

Run-ons and fragments

This "sentence" has no subject and no main verb, just three modifying phrases. One of them must be converted to a main clause, for example: "Mara ran all the way, …" or "Running all the way, Mara refused to stop … ."

Just last week, in the first elections held since the fall of the tyrant, my 85-year-old great grandfather has cast his first vote in over 50 years.

Verb tense

The only problem in this complex sentence is that there is no reason for the perfect tense ("has cast"); the simple past is correct. Ignore the intervening phrase, and it reads simply "Just last week, … grandfather … cast his first vote."

Uncommonly long-armed, most observers agreed that Rob Roy had a great advantage as a swordsman.

I read an essay where the author argued that no picketing should ever be permitted on government property.

Although she welcomed the news of this additional income, Shuping having been financially independent all her life.

The author decided to dedicate the novel to a ruthless tyrant during that period of political unrest, which annoys the publisher.

A good way to test the reliability of medical textbooks is by examining the credentials of its editorial boards.

Mary isn't concerned with what her admissions counselor told her about the test.

I read an essay where the author argued that no picketing should ever be permitted on government property.

Relative pronouns

Though common in conversation, the use of "where" to mean "in which" is incorrect. "Where" is only correctly used to refer to a location. The negative—"no picketing … ever"—is correctly expressed: it would be wrong if "never" were substituted for "ever."

Uncommonly long-armed, most observers agreed that Rob Roy had a great advantage as a swordsman.

Modifiers

Whenever you have an introductory modifying phrase, check whether the word it modifies follows it. In this case, "Rob Roy"—not the "observers"—should be the subject of the sentence and the first words after the opening phrase.

The author decided to dedicate the novel to a ruthless tyrant during that period of political unrest, which annoys the publisher.

Verb tense

The first action in this sentence occurred in the past, so the second verb should also be in the past ("annoyed") unless the sentence provides some reason for another tense. The phrase "decided to dedicate" is idiomatically correct.

Although she welcomed the news of this additional income, Shuping having been financially independent all her life.

Run-ons and fragments

The first clause here has a verb, but "Although" makes it a dependent clause; it can't be the main clause of the sentence. The second part of the sentence is missing a verb. You can fix it by changing "having been" to an active verb like "was" or "had been" (depending on the context).

Mary isn't concerned with what her admissions counselor told her about the test.

Idiom

In this context, the word "concerned" requires the preposition "about"—not "with"—to complete it. Note the clear and logical sequence of tenses: Mary "isn't" concerned (in the present) about what her counselor "told" her (in the past).

A good way to test the reliability of medical textbooks is by examining the credentials of its editorial boards.

Pronoun agreement

Here, the pronoun "its" is meant to refer to "textbooks"—so it should be the plural "their." Note, though, "editorial boards" is correctly plural to agree with "textbooks."

Due to the innovative wing design, this aircraft encounters scarcely no wind resistance even at the highest speeds.

Although we got up at 4 A.M., breakfast took so long that the sun had raised before we were able to pack the car and start our journey.

The author of what is possibly the ideal social novel, Jane Austen seeked to advance a recently evolved concept of the nature of fiction.

Anyone who misses the morning bus knows that they will be picked up by the van in the afternoon.

Of all the students in the senior class, Ephraim is the undoubtedly smarter, even though his grades do not reflect his ability.

The handwriting was so poor that Jana couldn't determine to who the letter was written.

Although we got up at 4 A.M., breakfast took so long that the sun had raised before we were able to pack the car and start our journey.

Diction

The sun "rises" (not "raises"), and the proper perfect-tense form of this irregular verb is "had risen." The phrase "so long that" is the correct idiom.

Due to the innovative wing design, this aircraft encounters scarcely no wind resistance even at the highest speeds.

Idiom

The adverb "scarcely" is an implicitly negative word, making the "no" a double negative, idiomatically incorrect in standard English. It should read "scarcely any wind resistance." The opening phrase is introduced logically by "due to."

Anyone who misses the morning bus knows that they will be picked up by the van in the afternoon.

Pronoun agreement

"Anyone" is singular, not plural, so the pronoun "they" doesn't agree with it. The correct pronoun would be he or she, depending on the context. Note that this sentence provides a hint: "knows" is the singular form. The sequence of tenses is clear and logical here.

The author of what is possibly the ideal social novel, Jane Austen seeked to advance a recently evolved concept of the nature of fiction.

Irregular verbs

You have to know the forms of the irregular verbs; the past of "seek" is "sought"—not "seeked." The phrase "concept of the nature of fiction" is idiomatically correct.

The handwriting was so poor that Jana couldn't determine to who the letter was written.

Pronoun case

A noun or pronoun in a prepositional phrase is never the subject; so "who" should be "whom." The construction "so poor that" is idiomatically correct.

Of all the students in the senior class, Ephraim is the undoubtedly smarter, even though his grades do not reflect his ability.

Comparative/superlative

The adjective "smarter" is comparative. When more than two things are compared, the superlative is used, so Ephraim is the "smartest." The adverb "undoubtedly" correctly modifies the adjective.

The excessive rain this summer had a bad affect on the wallpaper in our back porch.

Elspeth told Juanita that she couldn't finish her dinner.

The dispatcher having told Teri that, to succeed in this business, being fast is more significant than being correct.

The seven flavors of fruit drink all come in a different colored jar.

Hari wanted to undertake the challenging project, but was insecure that he could complete it on time.

We expect to adopt a new dog that is healthy and good-natured, but it is not likely to being purebred.

Elspeth told Juanita that she couldn't finish her dinner.

Ambiguity

Who couldn't finish her dinner? The pronouns are ambiguous because there are two people they might refer to. To fix this, we might repeat one name, or we might change the sentence structure to avoid using a pronoun: "Elspeth said that Juanita couldn't finish dinner."

The excessive rain this summer had a bad affect on the wallpaper in our back porch.

Diction

The word "affect" is a common verb meaning "influence or change," but the word needed here is the noun "effect" meaning "result." "Excessive" is the right word here, an adjective modifying "rain."

The seven flavors of fruit drink all come in a different colored jar.

Noun agreement

Each different flavor has a different colored jar—so there must be seven different colored jars, not one. Standing alone and in the singular "a different colored jar" is also illogical, since we don't know what the color is different from; "different colored jars" are clearly different from each other.

The dispatcher having told Teri that, to succeed in this business, being fast is more significant than being correct.

Run-ons and fragments

The main clause of the sentence should be "The dispatcher told Teri…" "Having told" is a modifier, not a verb. Although "being" is frequently misused in SAT sentences, it is correctly used here in a parallel structure.

We expect to adopt a new dog that is healthy and good-natured, but it is not likely to being purebred.

Idiom

The correct idiom is "likely to be," not "likely to being." "Healthy" and "good-natured" are both adjectives, correctly modifying the noun "dog."

Hari wanted to undertake the challenging project, but was insecure that he could complete it on time.

Diction

"Insecure" is not a synonym for "uncertain"—it means unsafe, unstable, or anxious, rather than just lacking certainty. The phrases "wanted to undertake" and "on time" are idiomatically correct.

Most of the class still are not participating in the writing competition and regular reminders from the teacher to encourage them to do so.

You'll love our new reclosable bottles of Spur. They are so delicious and refreshing.

Certainly the new furniture was professional looking. It was not well-suited to the space.

We wanted to have non-athletic student activities after school, too. Like a literary magazine, debating team, and chess club, among others.

For those of you who are afraid of flying, we should remember that fewer accidents occur in airplanes than in automobiles.

I often recall my mother's words when I go to Paris Park, it being one of the most luxuriant green spaces in our town.

You'll love our new reclosable bottles of Spur. They are so delicious and refreshing.

Run-ons and fragments

There are two problems here: The second sentence is a fragment that should be joined to the first, and "they" seems to refer to "bottles" instead of "Spur." Try "You'll love our new reclosable bottles of delicious and refreshing Spur."

Most of the class still are not participating in the writing competition and regular reminders from the teacher to encourage them to do so.

Transitions

Instead of the conjunction "and," this sentence needs a transition word like "despite" between its two halves, to clarifies the contrasted ideas. The subject "Most" correctly takes the plural verb.

We wanted to have non-athletic student activities after school, too. Like a literary magazine, debating team, and chess club, among others.

Run-ons and fragments

The second "sentence" is a fragment. Correct it by joining it to the first with a comma. "Like" is correctly used here, a preposition meaning "such as, for example."

Certainly the new furniture was professional looking. It was not well-suited to the space.

Transitions

These sentences name two qualities of the same thing, one positive and one negative. Therefore, the overall idea would be better conveyed by combining them with a transition word showing contrast, like "but" or "although."

I often recall my mother's words when I go to Paris Park, it being one of the most luxuriant green spaces in our town.

Wordiness

"It being" is never good SAT writing; these words can be simply omitted to make the second part of the sentence an appropriate modifying phrase describing "Paris Park."

For those of you who are afraid of flying, we should remember that fewer accidents occur in airplanes than in automobiles.

Pronoun agreement

Good SAT sentences don't change from "you" in the first half to "we" in the second. Note that "fewer" is used correctly, since "accidents" are countable.

All the readers found that Sandra's writing style was very different than Sarah's.

My sister and I disagreed about who would return the books at the library.

The first thing we had to do was clear the room. We couldn't move around in it.

We distributed lists of known violations, and everyone we met was urged by us to avoid the more flagrant scofflaw establishments.

Both individual freedoms as well as economic growth have improved rapidly since the fall of the dictatorship.

The cakes and cookies that we ordered to be delivered to the church fair were less expensive and far more attractive than Mayfair's Bakery.

My sister and I disagreed about who would return the books at the library.

Idiom

The only word wrong here is "at"—the books would be returned "to" the library, idiomatically. "My sister and I" (the subject) is correct at the beginning of the sentence.

All the readers found that Sandra's writing style was very different than Sarah's.

Idiom

The correct preposition with "different" is "from" ("than" can be used only if it is followed by a clause). Note that the past tense "found" is followed correctly by the past tense "was" because there is no reason for the tense to change.

We distributed lists of known violations, and everyone we met was urged by us to avoid the more flagrant scofflaw establishments.

Unnecessary passive

The sentence switches from the active voice to the passive, making it wordy. It should say "we distributed…, and we urged…" for conciseness and parallel structure.

The first thing we had to do was clear the room. We couldn't move around in it.

Transitions

To make the close relationship between these two sentences clearer, we could combine them with a semicolon. But they would be even clearer if combined with a transition word that states the relationship between them, like "because."

The cakes and cookies that we ordered to be delivered to the church fair were less expensive and far more attractive than Mayfair's Bakery.

Comparisons

The cakes in the first part of the sentence are compared to a bakery, rather than to cakes produced by that bakery. "Ordered to be delivered" is a good, idiomatic phrase, and, despite the intervening clause, the verb "were" agrees with its subject "cakes and cookies."

Both individual freedoms as well as economic growth have improved rapidly since the fall of the dictatorship.

Wordiness

The word "both" is redundant with "as well as"—you only need one or the other. The verb is correctly plural, because the subject is "individual freedoms," but remember that "as well as" does not make this a compound subject. If the subject were "individual freedom" the verb would be singular.

The statistics released today by the environmental study group makes our air quality seem worse than we anticipated.

Surprisingly, we found it easier to move the piano into the other room than getting the refrigerator to the other side of the kitchen.

We were planning for going to Stockholm that summer, but couldn't find an affordable hotel.

If you look at the packages careful, you'll find that the larger size washes fewer loads of laundry than the smaller one.

Unlike Colorado and Utah, New England's ski slopes are frequently icy, unpleasantly frigid, and overcrowded.

The president's economists recommended a tax reduction, convinced that the resulting increase in consumer spending would stimulate the economy.

Surprisingly, we found it easier to move the piano into the other room than getting the refrigerator to the other side of the kitchen.

Parallelism

Two actions are compared, and must be in parallel form: "to move the piano" and "to get the refrigerator." The adverb "Surprisingly" is correctly used.

The statistics released today by the environmental study group makes our air quality seem worse than we anticipated.

Subject-verb agreement

Because "statistics" is plural, the verb should be "make" instead of "makes"—even though the singular "study group" is the closest noun. Notice that the correct word for the comparison is "than"—not "then" as sometimes appears in students' essays.

If you look at the packages careful, you'll find that the larger size washes fewer loads of laundry than the smaller one.

Adjective/adverb

The adjective "careful" modifies the verb "look"—so it should be the adverb "carefully" instead. Note that "fewer" is correctly used, since the wash loads are countable.

We were planning for going to Stockholm that summer, but couldn't find an affordable hotel.

Idiom

The correct idiom is not "planning for going" but "planning to go" or "planning on going." The conjunction "but" makes a reasonable transition here, and "were planning" is parallel to "couldn't find."

The president's economists recommended a tax reduction, convinced that the resulting increase in consumer spending would stimulate the economy.

Modifiers

This sentence could be improved by moving the long modifying phrase at the end closer to the word it modifies ("economists"). "The president's economists, convinced that the resulting increase in consumer spending would stimulate the economy, …" It is idiomatically correct to say "recommended a tax reduction."

Unlike Colorado and Utah, New England's ski slopes are frequently icy, unpleasantly frigid, and overcrowded.

Comparisons

The comparison here is between "Colorado and Utah" on the one hand, and "ski slopes" on the other (the possessive "New England's" only modifies them). It should say "Unlike those of Colorado and Utah, …" or "New England has ski slopes that …" The modifiers at the end of the sentence are correctly used and in parallel form.

Each of the boys has their own camping equipment.

When he finally finished the grueling test, Pepi found it incredulous that it had only taken three hours.

Although we were better trained, the others ran so quick that we couldn't keep up with them.

Our team had to be disbanded when the pitcher moves out of state.

Max negotiating a contract that will improve conditions and be acceptable to the owners.

Every time I tried to reach Alice, she was either talking on the phone and out of her house.

When he finally finished the grueling test, Pepi found it incredulous that it had only taken three hours.

Diction

"Incredulous" means "not believing"—the word intended is "incredible" meaning "not believable." The past perfect "had taken" is used correctly, since that action was completed when Pepi "finished" the test.

Each of the boys has their own camping equipment.

Pronoun agreement

Not "boys" but "Each" is the subject of the sentence and the antecedent of the pronoun, so "their" should be "his." Note that the singular verb, agreeing with its singular subject, reinforces the point.

Our team had to be disbanded when the pitcher moves to another state.

Verb tenses

Since the team "had to be disbanded" in the past, the pitcher's move can't be in the present tense. It should be "moved." To "move out of" is idiomatically correct.

Although we were better trained, the others ran so quick that we couldn't keep up with them.

Adjective/adverb

The adjective "quick" can't correctly modify the verb "ran"—the adverb "quickly" should be used. The pronoun "we" is used clearly and consistently here.

Every time I tried to reach Alice, she was either talking on the phone and out of her house.

Idiom

The correct word to complete a phrase starting with "either" is "or"—not "and." The phrase "tried to reach" is idiomatically correct.

Max negotiating a contract that will improve conditions and be acceptable to the owners.

Run-ons and fragments

There is no verb here; we have to add "is" before "negotiating." Note that "improve conditions" and "be acceptable" may look different but are parallel.

Charlotte and me were best friends at camp, but we never see each other now.

Luke was the smarter boy in our class until Jeremy transferred in.

Each student must take responsibility for their own test preparation.

All the girls on the swim team want to be an Olympic champion.

We can always find the presents our mother hides if we look careful.

Mary, Linda, and I is going to travel in Europe this summer.

Luke was the smarter boy in our class until Jeremy transferred in.

Comparative/superlative

All the boys in the class are compared, and without a specified number, we assume there are more than two of them so "smarter" should be "smartest." "Until Jeremy transferred in" is idiomatically correct.

Charlotte and me were best friends at camp, but we never see each other now.

Pronoun case

The correct word is "I" rather than "me" since "Charlotte and I" is the subject of the sentence. The transition "but" is correctly used, since the end of the sentence contrasts with the beginning.

All the girls on the swim team want to be an Olympic champion.

Noun agreement

All the girls don't want to be the same champion—they want to be champions. The verb "want" is correctly plural to agree with the subject.

Each student must take responsibility for their own test preparation.

Pronoun agreement

The word "each" is singular, so "their" is incorrectly plural. In this case, "his" or "her" (or both) should be used. The phrase "responsibility for" is idiomatically correct.

Mary, Linda, and I is going to travel to Europe this summer.

Subject-verb agreement

"Mary, Linda, and I" is a compound subject, requiring a plural verb, "are." The pronoun "I" is correctly used, since it is part of the subject.

We could always find the presents that our mother had hidden if we looked careful.

Adjective/adverb

The word "careful" is used here to modify the verb "looked"—so it should be the adverb "carefully." The pronoun "that" correctly refers to the "presents."

I wasn't without an opinion; I just didn't want to be expressing it.

Tan's style of dressing was colorful, luxurious, and ostensible.

Before Wally had ate a bite of his dinner, the phone rang again.

If someone knows why Geoff isn't in class, he or she should leave the principal know.

Beth is more skilled at fiction writing rather than her sister Anya, to whom she dedicated her book.

Having a good time is more important than to win the game, as my coach always says when we lose.

Tan's style of dressing was colorful, luxurious, and ostensible.

Diction

What the writer means is "ostentatious," meaning "boastfully showy." "Ostensible" means "apparent, professed," which doesn't make sense here. The phrase "style of dressing" uses the idiomatically correct preposition.

I wasn't without an opinion, I just didn't want to be expressing it.

Wordiness

The verb should be simply "want to express"—"want to be expressing" is wordy and non-idiomatic. The two negatives at the beginning are correct, though, since the writer means she did have an opinion.

If anyone knows why Geoff isn't in class, he or she should leave the principal know.

Diction

The student who knows should "let" (not "leave") the principal know. Note that the pronouns "he or she" are correctly used with the singular "someone."

Before Wally had ate a bite of his dinner, the phone rang again.

Irregular verbs

The correct form of the verb "eat" in the perfect tenses is "eaten"—not "ate." But "rang" is the correct past form of the irregular verb "ring."

Having a good time is more important than to win the game, as my coach always says when we lose.

Parallel

Two things are compared here: "having a good time" and "to win the game"—so the second part should be in parallel form: "winning the game." The verb tenses are correctly all present tense.

Beth is more skilled at fiction writing rather than her sister Anya, to whom she dedicated her book.

Idiom

The correct completion of the idiom is "more…than," not "more…rather than." Beth is more skilled than her sister. Note the correct pronoun case: as the object of the preposition, we use "whom" rather than "who."

In the coming months, Antarctica will experience the most extremest weather conditions ever known on the planet.

As we walked further into the jungle, we found that our clothes, as well too all of our equipment and food supplies, were being coated with sap.

Although she worked the same number of hours this month, Ilsa was paid less of money than last month.

Speaking before the graduating class, nothing human should be alien to us was the advice Maya Angelou gave.

Amir knows more about soccer than the rest of us because of being his favorite sport.

Fast food hamburgers are quicker and easier than home-cooked meals, but the greater is its cost.

As we walked further into the jungle, we found that our clothes, as well too all of our equipment and food supplies, were being coated with sap.

Idiom

The correct phrase is "as well as"—not "as well too." Note the subject-verb agreement. Although this is not a compound subject, "our clothes" are still plural.

In the coming months, Antarctica will experience the most extremest weather conditions ever known on the planet.

Comparative/superlative

The superlative is formed either by adding –*est* or by using "most"—not both; here the correct form is "most extreme." The future tense is correctly used to refer to what will happen in "the coming months."

Speaking before the graduating class, nothing human should be alien to us was the advice Maya Angelou gave.

Modifiers

The opening phrase must modify the noun that follows it. Since Maya Angelou was speaking, the sentence should end "Maya Angelou advised us that nothing human should be alien to us." The idiom "alien to" is correct.

Although she worked the same number of hours this month, Ilsa was paid less of money than last month.

Idiom

The preposition "of" doesn't belong in the phrase "paid less money." The verb tenses are correctly consistent in this sentence.

A fast food hamburger is quicker, easier, and more popular than home-cooked meals, but the greater is its cost.

Idiom

The sentence is awkward and unidiomatic; we would say "but it costs more." Note the correct parallelism in "quicker, easier, and more popular."

Amir knows more about soccer than the rest of us because of being his favorite sport.

Idiom

"Because of being" isn't idiomatic English; we say "because it is." The comparison "more about soccer than the rest of us" is unambiguous, though you could also say "than the rest of us do."

Jen, Mia, and Em shared in common a determination to become famous rock trios.

Indira is best known for her dancing, and her singing was well received at the concert.

I like to read the sports section of the papers first, my sister starts with the business section.

The neighbor's chimney does not cause as much smoke like the one in my house does.

Hundreds of bananas were dropped onto the road, and they had to stop traffic to clean up.

On weekends, more fans arrive at the stadium from the subways than the parking lots.

Indira is best known for her dancing, and her singing was well received at the concert.

Transitions

The sentence suggests a contrast, which would be better expressed by using "but" to start the second half. The superlative "best" is correctly used, since the sentence compares all the things Indira is known for, not just the two named in the sentence.

Jen, Mia, and Em shared a determination to become famous rock trios.

Noun agreement

In this case, the three presumably want to be in the same trio, not several. "Shared a determination" is idiomatically correct.

The neighbor's chimney does not cause as much smoke like the one in my house does.

Comparisons

The correct form of the comparison is "as much...as," rather than "as much...like." The things compared are correct, however: the "neighbor's chimney" and "the one in my house."

I like to read the sports section of the papers first, my sister starts with the business section.

Run-ons and fragments

There are two main clauses here, so the comma should be a period or a semicolon, or a conjunction should be added (like "but"). The phrase "starts with" is correct.

On weekends, more fans arrive at the stadium from the subways than the parking lots.

Comparisons

We are comparing fans "from the subways" with those "from the parking lots." The preposition "from" should be repeated. The phrase "at the stadium" is correct.

Hundreds of bananas were dropped onto the road, and they had to stop traffic to clean up.

Ambiguity

The pronoun "they" has nothing to refer to but the bananas, which are doing the cleanup themselves, apparently. Replace the pronoun with the right noun, something like "the emergency crew." The phrases "onto the road" and "to clean up" are both idiomatically correct.

Having run to answer the phone, that the caller hung up just as he arrived irritated Zed.

The main reasons the workers gave for the strike is that they are paid to little and have too few holidays.

The tourists, coming so far, didn't want to leave without seeing the statue.

After ten minutes in the sauna, he was as soaked as if swimming instead.

The beneficial effects of sunlight on depression is generally acknowledged.

The problem troubling Joel, which was whether to go to the game or to the party.

The main reasons the workers gave for the strike is that they are paid to little and have too few holidays.

Subject-verb agreement

In complex sentences, be sure you know what subjects and verbs match up. The "main reasons" are plural, so "is" should be "are." The other verbs all match their subjects and are in appropriate tenses.

Having run to answer the phone, that the caller hung up just as he arrived irritated Zed.

Modifiers

Who ran to answer the phone? Zed; so he should be the subject of the main clause. "Zed was irritated that the caller hung up just as he arrived." The verbs in the sentence are logical and consistent.

After ten minutes in the sauna, he was as soaked as if swimming instead.

Verb tenses

This sentence compares how soaked he was to how soaked he would have been if he "had been swimming" instead. The past perfect is correct because the swimming would have been completed at the time of the comparison, which occurs in the past. The comparison is correctly structure with the words "as…as if."

The exhausted tourists, coming this far, didn't want to leave without seeing the statue.

Idiom

This sentence is difficult to understand as written; the logical form is "The tourists, having come so far, …" The adjective "exhausted" correctly modifies the noun "tourists."

The problem troubling Joel, which was whether to go to the game or to the party.

Run-ons and fragments

There is no independent clause here, so we have a fragment. Deleting the comma and "which" would correct it, making the subject "problem" and the verb "was." Notice the correct parallel structure at the end of the sentence.

The beneficial effects of sunlight on depression is generally acknowledged.

Subject-verb agreement

The subject is "effects" (not "depression") so the verb should be "are." The adverb "generally" correctly modifies "acknowledged."

Archy will be in the spelling bee, for his grades in this have been excellent.

Being as she is the only teacher available, Sara will lead the session.

The novelist never wrote about family life, however he regarded it as too personal.

Back in 1990, the group thought they had a song that would have launched their career.

Our choir, consisting of 50 singers, and is led by a former opera star.

Whether Pepe ate the cookies or did not remains uncertain, but he had the opportunity.

Being as she is the only teacher available, Sara will lead the session.

Wordiness

Just drop the first four words and you have a clearer, shorter sentence. Phrases like "being as she is" will never be right on the SAT. The verb tenses make sense here.

Archy will be in the spelling bee, for his grades in this have been excellent.

Ambiguity

The pronoun "this" is intended to refer to "spelling," but that noun doesn't appear in the sentence—the only noun it could refer to is "bee" ("spelling" is a modifier). The transition "for" correctly identifies the relationship between the two parts of the sentence.

Back in 1990, the group thought they had a song that would have launched their career.

Verb tense

The correct form of the verb for the logic of this sentence is just "that would launch their career." The use of the past tense ("thought") is correct, since this was "back in 1990."

The novelist never wrote about his family life, however he regarded it as too personal.

Transitions

The second part of the sentence explains the first half; the word joining them should make that clear. "However" should be "because." The phrase "regarded…as" is idiomatically correct.

Whether Pepe ate the cookies or did not remains uncertain, but he had the opportunity.

Wordiness

"Whether Pepe ate…or did not" needlessly repeats the information that it "remains uncertain." One or the other is all that's needed. "That Pepe ate the cookies remains uncertain." The second clause uses the right transition and the right verb tense.

Our choir, consisting of 50 singers, and is led by a former opera star.

Run-ons and fragments

The writer intended to have two verbs referring to the same subject, but the first is not a verb ("consisting" is a modifier). Change "consisting" to "consists" and delete the comma to correct this. Otherwise, it's fine to have the subject, "our choir," appear only once—it would be wordy to add a pronoun or repeat the subject.

Our team beat Johnson High's team that year, even so, we did not win again until today.

The Jeffersons have switched to DSL long before their neighbors got any Internet connection.

Sada would like to go to Europe, but the airfare is unable to be afforded by her.

Ted's cookies are always delicious considering that he uses only the freshest ingredients.

Arlene, a member of our track team, whose sense of humor rivals that of the class clown.

Just as Cynthia helped with the baking and Mike with the cleaning up, Carly's contribution was to help build the piñata.

The Jeffersons have switched to DSL long before their neighbors got any Internet connection.

Verb tenses

There are two events, one in the past ("got") and one that occurred before that. The past perfect is needed ("had switched") rather than "have switched." The pronoun "their" correctly refers to "the Jeffersons."

Our team beat Johnson High's team that year, even so, we did not win again until today.

Transitions

As written, this is a run-on sentence, but the logical correction is to change "even so" (the wrong contrast words) to "but" to express the correct relationship between the two parts of the sentence. Verb tenses are logical.

Ted's cookies are always delicious considering that he uses only the freshest ingredients.

Transitions

What is the logical connection between the cookies being delicious and the ingredients used? Cause-and-effect. The connector "considering that" should be replaced with "because." The adjective "delicious" correctly modifies the noun "cookies."

Sada would like to go to Europe, but the airfare is unable to be afforded by her.

Unnecessary passive

We could call this wordy, but the wordiness is caused by the passive construction. "Sada would like to go to Europe, but can't afford the airfare." The phrase "like to go" is idiomatically correct.

Just as Cynthia helped with the baking and Mike with the cleaning up, Carly's contribution was to help build the piñata.

Idiom

The phrase "just as" at the beginning of this sentence must be completed with "so" at the start of the second clause, and Carly's work should parallel Cynthia's and Mike's. "Just as Cynthia helped with the baking and Mike with the cleaning up, so Carly helped build the piñata." The contributions of Cynthia and Mike are correctly parallel in form.

Arlene, a member of our track team, whose sense of humor rivals that of the class clown.

Run-ons and fragments

We have a subject and a modifying clause—no main verb. We might fix this by saying "Arlene is a member of our track team whose sense of humor rivals that of the class clown." The phrase "rivals that of…" is idiomatically correct.

Houston, while being about 60 miles inland, is America's third largest foreign-trade port.

Most team members are motivated of team spirit, but some are interested only in personal glory.

These keys are invaluable because it can't be duplicated.

This handmade walnut clock is the only one of a kind in North America.

Christy Brown, his disability has influenced his entire life, tells his story in *My Left Foot*.

She is absent when the class decided to do the play, so Marta is afraid she won't get a good part.

Most team members are motivated of team spirit, but some are interested only in personal glory.

Idiom

The correct phrase is "motivated by" team spirit. The phrase "interested only in personal glory" is idiomatically correct.

Houston, while being about 60 miles inland, is America's third largest foreign-trade port.

Transitions

"While being" is a poor connector here; the meaning is clearer if we change it to "although." The superlative "largest" is correctly used to compare all of America's ports.

This handmade walnut clock is the only one of a kind in North America.

Idiom

The idiom intended is "one of its kind." "One of a kind" is another idiom, meaning "unique." "Handmade" and "walnut" are correctly used to modify "clock."

These keys are invaluable because it is the only set and can't be duplicated.

Pronoun agreement

The pronoun "it" must refer to "these keys," so it and the verb should be plural: " they are." "Invaluable" (meaning, paradoxically, "priceless or useful") is the correct word here.

She is absent when the class decided to do the play, so Marta is afraid she won't get a good part.

Verb tense

Although the second half of the sentence is in the present tense, the first part is not—"the class decided." So the first "is" should be "was." The phrase "decided to do" is the correct idiom.

Christy Brown, his disability has influenced his entire life, tells his story in My Left Foot.

Run-ons and fragments

There are two complete independent clauses here, joined badly. By changing the first "his" to "whose" we can make that clause dependent and correct the sentence. "Has influenced" is the correct tense for action that continues into the present.

In those classes in whom all students are reading at grade level, few discipline problems occur.

The poll Cindy refers to, which was prepared jointly by she and the committee, was flawed.

A system for improving test scores is not only desirable but of necessity in all classes.

In making your recommendation, has you taken into account the cost involved?

It is harder to explain the directions to the convention center than showing you the way.

I'm not sure that I know exactly how a pogo stick is rode.

The poll Cindy refers to, which was prepared jointly by she and the committee, was flawed.

Pronoun case

When a pronoun follows a preposition, it shouldn't be in the subjective case; the report "was prepared jointly by her and the committee." The relative pronoun "which" is used correctly to refer to the report.

In those classes in whom all students are reading at grade level, few discipline problems occur.

Pronoun agreement

The relative pronoun "whom" shouldn't be used to refer to classes; it should say "in which." The phrase "at grade level" uses the correct preposition.

In making your recommendation, have you taken into account the higher cost involved?

Subject-verb agreement

Don't be confused just because the verb precedes its subject. The subject is "you" and the verb should be "have"—not "has." "Taken into account" is idiomatically correct.

A system for improving test scores is not only desirable but of necessity in all classes.

Idiom

The idiom "of necessity" means "because it is necessary." The correct word here is simply the adjective "necessary." A "system for improving" is idiomatically correct.

I'm not sure that I know exactly how a pogo stick is rode.

Irregular verbs

The perfect-tense form of the verb "to ride" is "ridden"—not "rode" (the simple past tense). The adverb "exactly" correctly modifies the adverb "how."

It is harder to explain the directions to the convention center than showing you the way.

Comparisons

The writer compares the difficulty "to explain" something with "showing" it. The items compared should be parallel in form, so "showing" should be "to show." The comparative "harder" is correctly used to compare two items.

Meg was satisfactory, for the most part, with her apartment, but wanted new curtains.

I thought on taking a position at my family's law firm, but didn't like the hours.

Della's preoccupation on finding her lost ring caused her to arrive in class late.

Stubbornness appears to be the one fault that Pete and me have in common.

Impressed over the new design that Ann submitted, the company awarded the job to her.

Bobby fell on the way home, lost his homework, and had a fight with his friend, which made him sad.

I thought on taking a position at my family's law firm, but didn't like the hours.

Idiom

We don't "think on" in formal writing; we "think about" something. The contrast word "but" is the right transition between the two parts of this sentence.

Meg was satisfactory, for the most part, with her apartment, but wanted new curtains.

Diction

Meg used the wrong word. The curtains may be "satisfactory," but Meg was "satisfied." "For the most part" is a correct idiomatic phrase.

Stubbornness appears to be the one fault that Pete and me have in common.

Pronoun case

"Pete and me" is the subject of the clause at the end of the sentence, so it should be "Pete and I" instead. The verb, "have," correctly agrees with this compound subject.

Della's preoccupation on finding her lost ring caused her to arrive in class late.

Idiom

The correct preposition with "preoccupation" is "with"—not "on." The verb form "to arrive" is idiomatically correct with "caused."

Bobby fell on the way home, lost his homework, and had a fight with his friend, which made him sad.

Ambiguity

Was Bobby sad because of his fight, or did all three events contribute to his sadness? Using "all of which" (instead of just "which") could clarify.

Impressed over the new design that Ann submitted, the company awarded the job to her.

Idiom

Once more, the wrong preposition is used; we say "impressed by" or "impressed with." The pronoun "her" is used correctly to refer to "Ann."

The information on job-training opportunities were sent to the wrong address.

Fine art, such as Michelangelo's *David* and DaVinci's *Mona Lisa*, succeeds by their speaking directly to each viewer.

Ted is very popular at school considering that he is both cheerful and helpful.

The story of Romeo and Juliet was popular in the nineteenth century, where it was the subject of an opera and a ballet.

Absorbed in the fascinating discussion, the time passed quickly.

Terry spoke with Andy when he was waiting in the hallway.

Fine art, such as Michelangelo's David and DaVinci's Mona Lisa, succeeds by their speaking directly to each viewer.

.

Pronoun agreement

The sentence says "fine art succeeds by speaking directly"—the pronoun "their" is unnecessary; if you do include a pronoun, it should be "its" to agree with the antecedent, "art." The verb "succeeds" correctly agrees with is subject.

The information on job-training opportunities were sent to the wrong address.

Subject-verb agreement

The subject isn't "opportunities"—it's "information"—so the verb should be singular. The passive is appropriate, since the "information" is the focus of the sentence (and we don't know who did the sending).

The story of Romeo and Juliet was popular in the nineteenth century, where it was the subject of both an opera and a ballet.

Diction

The word "where" shouldn't be used to refer to anything but location. The correct word is "when." The comparison is set up correctly with "both…and" and the items are parallel.

Ted is very popular at school considering that he is both cheerful and helpful.

Transitions

The sentence offer two reasons for Ted's popularity; the correct transition here is "because"—not "considering that." The adverb "very" correctly modifies the adjective "popular."

Terry spoke with Andy when he was waiting in the hallway.

Ambiguity

Terry and Andy may both be male; which does the pronoun "he" refer to? We can clarify by rewording, for example: "While Andy waited in the hallway, Terry spoke with him." Consistent use of the past tense is correct here.

Absorbed in the fascinating discussion, the time passed quickly.

Modifiers

The subject the intended to modify with this opening phrase doesn't appear in the sentence at all. We have to add a proper subject, such as "John found that the time passed quickly." The adverb "quickly" correctly modifies the verb "passed."

The family is still debating whether Mike's talent for whistling is a blessing or is it a curse.

We are supplying the warmest blankets to those refugees which need them most.

Elron was afraid that the crowd growing impatient with the prolonged delay.

The jury should not make its decision before it seen all the evidence.

Money is certainly important, it has never ensured that anyone will be happy.

Although the constant roar of machinery left our ears ringing, but we enjoyed the tour of the factory.

We are supplying the warmest blankets to those refugees which need them most.

Pronoun agreement

The relative pronoun "which" can't be used to refer to people; we can replace it with "who." Notice that both "warmest" and "most" are correctly superlative, since many are compared.

The family is still debating whether Mike's talent for whistling is a blessing or is it a curse.

Parallel

The items compared are "is a blessing" and "is a curse." They should be parallel in form, so the words "is it" are unnecessary. The comparison is properly structured with "whether…or."

The jury should not make its decision before it seen all the evidence.

Irregular verbs

The correct form of the irregular verb "to see" is "has seen" (or the simple present can be used). The preposition "before" is the right transition between these two clauses, making the second dependent.

Elron was afraid that the crowd growing impatient with the prolonged delay.

Run-ons and fragments

A clause should follow "that," but no verb is provided here. "Growing" is a modifier. The adjective "prolonged" correctly modifies the noun "delay.

Although the constant roar of machinery left our ears ringing, but we enjoyed the tour of the factory.

Transitions

Too many transitions can be just as bad as too few. We need either "although" or "but"—not both. The "roar of machinery" is idiomatically correct.

Money is certainly important, it has never ensured that anyone will be happy.

Run-ons and fragments

These two independent clauses can't be combined with just a comma. Either an appropriate transition (like "yet") or a semicolon should be used between them. The phrase "ensured that" is idiomatically correct.

Since some of us wanted to wait for Jorge, but others set off for the park.

The children wore sneakers to class which the principal disapproved of.

Stravinsky's masterpiece is at once disorienting because of its unusual structure but its inventiveness is a pure delight.

Mr. Smith bought a boat for his family, which he couldn't afford.

Many people think starches are bad for their health, consequently, some of them avoid all kinds of bread.

Karla won both events, but the prizes weren't given to her until the next day.

The children wore sneakers to class, which the principal disapproved of.

Ambiguity

Did the principal disapprove of these particular sneakers or the fact that sneakers were worn at all? Reorganize or reword ambiguous sentences to make your meaning clear. The verb tenses are correctly consistent here.

Since some of us wanted to wait for Jorge, but others set off for the park.

Transitions

The problem here is too many transitions; the contrast transition "but" is appropriate, but "since" is unnecessary at the start of this sentence. Delete it. The preposition "for" is correct with "set off."

Mr. Smith bought a boat for his family, which he couldn't afford.

Modifiers

What was Mr. Smith unable to afford? It might be both his family and the boat, but presumably all the writer had in mind was the boat. The modifier should be placed next to the word modified. "Bought" is the correct, past form of the irregular verb "to buy."

Stravinsky's masterpiece is at once disorienting because of its unusual structure and its inventiveness is a pure delight.

Comparisons

The items compared should be in parallel form; the end of the sentence should be "and delightful because of its inventiveness." The structure "is at once…and" is correct structure for the comparison.

Karla won both events, but the prizes weren't given to her until the next day.

Unnecessary passive

Karla won the events and received her prizes—there is no reason not to keep her the subject of the second clause. "Karla won both events, but didn't receive her prizes until the next day." "Until the next day" is idiomatically correct.

Many people think starches are bad for their health, consequently, some of them avoid all kinds of bread.

Run-ons and fragments

There are two full sentences here. There should be a period or a semicolon before the word "consequently" (which is an appropriate transition to show the cause-and-effect relationship here).

Instructions:

These cards review basic principals of essay writing and some recommended strategies.

The SAT graders won't be looking for any particular essay form, but you can more easily and reliably build a clear, organized essay if you use a methodical approach and stick with proven structures.

What are the 4 steps for writing essays methodically?

What is the single most important rule of SAT essay writing?

What should your plan contain before you start to write?

What are the four basic criteria on which the essay is scored?

What kind of vocabulary is best to use in the essay?

TOWF: Think, Organize, Write, Proofread

Your plan should

(1) list all examples you will use and which paragraph you will cover them in, and

(2) identify what will be in your introduction and conclusion.

Answer the question!

(1) Use formal, descriptive language; avoid slang.

(2) Use words from the prompt to tie your essay to the assignment.

(3) Add some SAT vocabulary words if possible.

(1) Did it address the assignment?

(2) Is it organized?

(3) Is it sufficiently detailed?

(4) Is it well written?

What are two functions of a Thesis Statement?

What are five reliable ways to begin a piece of writing?

Define Paragraph Coherence.

Define Paragraph Unity.

What are the five ways to end a piece of writing?

Where should the Thesis Statement appear in the essay?

(1) Share a striking fact, (2) describe something, (3) ask a question, (4) tell a story, or (5) use a quotation or dialogue.

It keeps the writer focused on the main idea and lets the reader know what the paper is about.

Paragraph Unity means all sentences relate to the main idea of the paragraph.

Paragraph Coherence means details are presented in a clear, sensible order (chronologically or in order of importance, for instance).

It can be the first sentence of the essay, but it's generally most effective in the last sentence of the first paragraph. It can be restated in the first or last sentence of the last paragraph.

Restate the main idea, ask a question, make a recommendation, end with the last event, or generalize about your information.

Name five types of details to support a paragraph.

What is a Topic Sentence?

What are the two purposes of a Topic Sentence?

How should a paragraph be developed?

What kinds of examples should be used in your essay?

What simple words and phrases can make it easy for the reader to follow your reasoning in an essay?

Where the main idea of a paragraph is expressed.

Facts and statistics, sensory details, anecdotes, examples, and quotations.

Develop each paragraph by giving details in support of the Topic Sentence.

It helps the writer focus on the most important idea and helps the reader understand what the paragraph is about.

Transition words, like those relied on in Critical Reading, help the reader navigate your essay.

Any examples are fine—personal anecdotes, historical or current events, the arts or literature. Just avoid controversial issues that might offend your readers or topics that make **you** too emotional to write clearly.

What should you focus on when you proofread your essay on test day?

Name four ways to help ensure variety in your essay's sentence structure.

What are three ways to avoid wordiness in your essay?

Other than the Thesis Statement, what are the two most important sentences in your essay?

What are three common errors you should avoid in your last paragraph?

If you have to make corrections on test day, how should you make them?

(1) Vary the length of sentences. (2) Begin some sentences with modifiers. (3) Begin some sentences with phrases or dependent clauses. (4) Use transition words at the beginning of sentences or to combine one or more sentences.

Be sure you expressed your ideas clearly. Add transition words—or even full sentences, if necessary—to make your ideas easy to understand.

The first sentence because it makes the first impression, and the last sentence because it will be freshest in the readers' minds as they grade.

(1) Reduce a sentence to a clause, (2) reduce a clause to a phrase, (3) reduce a phrase to a single word.

Neatly and with a minimum of marking. Put a single line through words you are deleting. Use an asterisk (*) or caret (^) to show where additional words should be inserted.

(1) Don't introduce a new idea or afterthought. (2) Don't announce that you're going to conclude. (3) Don't apologize for your work.

What are three ways that the SAT essay is different from other essays you have written in school or for homework?

How is handwriting an essay in 30 minutes different from writing on a word processor.

What are two important qualities of a good introduction?

When should you start a new paragraph?

What are some transition words or phrases to indicate contrast?

What are some transition words or phrases to indicate examples?

You can't simply start writing, expecting to make substantial revisions, in your handwritten essay on test day. So plan your essay completely and think about each sentence before you start to write.

(1) You don't have any choice of topic (so be sure to answer the question).

(2) You don't have time to rewrite (so write carefully the first time).

(3) You don't have time to research the topic (but remember, you aren't graded on the accuracy of your facts).

Each new idea should be in a new paragraph. In particular, your introduction and conclusion should be separate paragraphs, and start a new paragraph (1) to move from one point to another, (2) to show a change in time period or location, (3) to discuss a new step or task, and (4) to emphasize an idea.

It grabs the interest of the reader, and it gives the reader a sense of what to expect in the essay.

For example, for instance, namely, specifically

Although, but, despite, even though, however, in contrast, instead, meanwhile, nevertheless, on the contrary, on the other hand, still, whereas, yet

What are some transition words to signal conclusions?

What are some transition words to signal concession to the other side of an issue?

What are some transition words to signal cause and effect?

What are a few simple rules that can help you keep your writing clear?

What should you do if your handwriting is difficult to read?

Admittedly, certainly, granted, naturally, of course

As a result, consequently, in conclusion, in other words, in summary, therefore, thus

(1) Generally, state your ideas actively instead
of passively, and positively instead of negatively.

(2) Remember the rules you learned for the multiple-choice questions.

Accordingly, as a result, because, consequently, since, so, then, therefore

(3) Don't use sentence structures or vocabulary that you aren't sure of.

Practice writing more clearly, if you have time to improve. Or practice printing your essays. Legibility definitely counts.

Brainstorming

Instructions:

You won't have much time to brainstorm on test day, but brainstorming in advance can arm you with ideas suitable to a wide variety of prompts.

There are two types of Brainstorming cards:

Some offer brief quotes for you to respond to. The quotes you will see on test day will probably be longer, but can and should be reduced to statements as simple as these.

Other cards prompt you to compile information about the interests, knowledge, and personal experiences that you can use as examples in your essay. They also prompt you for the kind of detail, reasoning, or vocabulary that help build strong essays.

Brainstorming

"Those who have freedom must also have self-restraint."

—Do you agree or disagree? Think of two or three examples.

Brainstorming

What is your favorite movie? What two or three SAT words apply to it? Name three events that take place in it.

Brainstorming

Think of a book you've enjoyed reading within the last two or three years. What was it about? What did you like about it?

Brainstorming

"Technological advances are making the world smaller every day."

—Do you agree or disagree? Think of two or three examples.

Brainstorming

"It is sometimes necessary to keep secrets."

—Do you agree or disagree? Think of two or three examples.

Notes

_____
_____
_____
_____
_____
_____
_____
_____
_____
_____

Using the Brainstorming Cards

Unlike most flashcards, these have no answers on the reverse. As in the SAT essay itself, there are no right answers.

Note your best examples on the reverse of the card. Use these to further develop those ideas when you use the card again, and to help keep those ideas fresh in your mind as you approach Test Day.

Notes

_____
_____
_____
_____
_____
_____
_____
_____
_____
_____
_____

Notes

_____
_____
_____
_____
_____
_____
_____
_____
_____

Notes

_____
_____
_____
_____
_____
_____
_____
_____
_____
_____

Notes

_____
_____
_____
_____
_____
_____
_____
_____
_____
_____

Brainstorming

"Censorship is sometimes justified."

—Do you agree or disagree? Think of two or three examples.

Brainstorming

List five things that you have accomplished over the last five years—not necessarily those for which you have received recognition, just things you are proud of.

Brainstorming

Name one or two events in your life that seemed insignificant at the time, but took on greater meaning later. Think about why.

Brainstorming

"Life's important lessons are not learned in school."

—Do you agree or disagree? Think of two or three examples.

Brainstorming

"Heroes are everyday people."

—Do you agree or disagree? Think of two or three examples.

Brainstorming

"The greatest griefs are those we cause ourselves."

—Do you agree or disagree? Think of two or three examples.

Notes

Notes

Notes

Notes

Notes

Notes

Brainstorming

Remember a time when someone whose opinion you respect gave you a good piece of advice (on any subject). What were the circumstances? What was the advice, and how did it change you?

Brainstorming

Who do you believe should be considered the most important person of the Twentieth Century? Think of several adjectives that describe that person.

Brainstorming

"Don't judge a person until you've walked a mile in his moccasins."

—Do you agree or disagree? Think of two or three examples.

Brainstorming

"Every great artist started as an amateur."

—Do you agree or disagree? Think of two or three examples.

Brainstorming

What event has been the most satisfying experience in your life? Was it something that happened to you or to someone else, or was it something you did? Was it planned or was it luck?

Brainstorming

List three people—whether real or fictional, living or dead, famous or a personal friend—whom you respect and admire. Think about why. What SAT words describe them?

Notes

Notes

Notes

Notes

Notes

Notes

Brainstorming

"The greatest part of our happiness or misery depends on our dispositions, not our circumstances."

—Do you agree or disagree? Think of two or three examples.

Brainstorming

"A sure way to fail is to try to please everybody."

—Do you agree or disagree? Think of two or three examples.

Brainstorming

What events in your life during the last five years have seemed most important to you? Why were they important?

Brainstorming

What is your favorite sport? What are three of its important qualities?

Brainstorming

Think of a problem you believe you know a solution to. What facts indicate that this problem exists? What is your solution, and how does it address those facts?

Brainstorming

Think of a time when you really wanted to convince someone else to do something. How did you choose your arguments? What arguments worked?

Notes

Notes

Notes

Notes

Notes

Notes

Brainstorming

List three to five things about which you consider yourself very knowledgeable. Don't limit yourself to academic subjects, but include hobbies, games—anything.

Brainstorming

What songs are your favorites, or what song has made a lasting impression on you? Choose one or two SAT words that describe it (or them).

Brainstorming

What do you consider a major scientific discovery made within your lifetime? What events demonstrate its importance?

Brainstorming

"Lying can be justified."

Do you agree or disagree? Think of two or three examples.

Brainstorming

What are your most important extracurricular or community activities (whether voluntary or involuntary)? Why is each important?

Brainstorming

What major historical event is the one you know the most about? Why did you learn about it? Does it have any significance for your own life?

Notes

Notes

Notes

Notes

Notes

Notes

Brainstorming

"A people is defined by its villains and its heroes."

—Do you agree or disagree? Think of two or three examples.

Brainstorming

"A real friend walks in when the rest of the world walks out on you."

—Do you agree or disagree? Think of two or three examples.

Brainstorming

Think of a book or article that changed the way you thought about something. How did you think before and how do you think now? How did it convince you?

Brainstorming

Think of an event that is important to you. What happened? Where? When? How and why did it happen? What happened after it that proves its importance?

Brainstorming

"It is human nature to seek knowledge."

—Do you agree or disagree? Think of two or three examples.

Brainstorming

Think of a friend who talked you into doing something you originally didn't want to do. Why were you convinced? Were you right to change your mind?

Notes

Notes

Notes

Notes

Notes

Notes

Brainstorming

What is your favorite course in school? What qualities about it appeal to you? Think of the single most memorable event that occurred in that course.

Brainstorming

"Slow and steady wins the race."

—Do you agree or disagree? Think of two or three examples.

Brainstorming

"Style is more important than substance."

—Do you agree or disagree? Think of two or three examples.

Brainstorming

What painting or sculpture can you recall that made a lasting impression on you? Choose one or two SAT words that describe it (or them).

Brainstorming

"Every obstacle is an opportunity."

—Do you agree or disagree? Think of two or three examples.

Brainstorming

"Give someone a fish and he eats today; teach someone to fish and she eats everyday."

—Do you agree or disagree? Think of two or three examples.

Notes

Notes

Notes

Notes

Notes

Notes

Brainstorming

"A free society is one in which it is safe to be unpopular."

—Do you agree or disagree? Think of two or three examples.

Brainstorming

"We are what we do most of the time, not what we do occasionally."

—Do you agree or disagree? Think of two or three examples.

Brainstorming

"Necessity is the mother of invention."

—Do you agree or disagree? Think of two or three examples.

Brainstorming

"Even a journey of a thousand miles must be started with a single step."

—Do you agree or disagree? Think of two or three examples.

Brainstorming

Think of something that you enjoyed learning (it doesn't have to be an academic subject). What made the learning enjoyable?

Brainstorming

Name a book or work of art that surprised you when you first encountered it. What was surprising about it? Did it change your view of art or literature?

Notes

Notes

Notes

Notes

Notes

Notes

Brainstorming

Think of a time when you recognized how important a friend or family member was to you. What were the circumstances? How has it affected you?

Brainstorming

"Beauty is only skin deep."

—Do you agree or disagree? Think of two or three examples.

Brainstorming

"Luck is a word we use to explain the success of those we don't like."

—Do you agree or disagree? Think of two or three examples.

Brainstorming

Who are your favorite musicians? Think of three to five adjectives to describe them. Think of three adjectives to describe how you feel about their music.

Brainstorming

What is your favorite book? Name three characters in it, and three adjectives to describe them.

Brainstorming

What are the two things you have in your pockets or schoolbag that you believe would tell others the most about who you are?

Notes

Notes

Notes

Notes

Notes

Notes